God Moment Miracles

Blessings Disguised
as
Hardship

Ann Smith Hill

God Moment Miracles
Blessings Disguised as Hardship

ISBN-13: 978-1494234966 (CreateSpace-Assigned)
ISBN-10: 1494234963
BISAC: Religion / Inspirational

Published by Ann Smith Hill
Franklinton, LA 70438
Email: snannaann@yahoo.com

Library of Congress Control No. 2014901341

Printed by CreateSpace
Available at Amazon in Paperback and Kindle

Credits
Every attempt has been made to credit the sources of copyrighted material used in this book. If any such acknowledgment has been inadvertently omitted, receipt of such information would be appreciated.

God Moment Miracles

Blessings Disguised
as
Hardship

Ann Smith Hill

An
Ann Smith Hill
Publication

Table of Contents

Acknowledgements

So many amazing people have contributed to the story which unfolds in this book. Over the years, these stories were in the form of a journal that has slowly been shaped into this book. I have encountered many beautiful people who have encouraged me, given me feedback and nudged me to continue when I questioned whether I should go forward with this endeavor.

First of all, I must acknowledge Jesus Christ, who is not only my Savior, but a friend who I can go to at any time, day or night; who allows me to cry out to Him for strength when I feel I can go no further.

Thanks to my husband, Joel, who has been with me through some of my deepest times of grieving. Having lost a daughter at the age of 14 in an automobile accident, his empathy was evident as I laid my two sons to rest.

I would like to thank my church family who prays with us and does not grow weary of the ongoing needs of our family. Rev. Carl Freeman, Rev. Randall Garcia, Rev. Jimmy Van Winkle, Rev. Paul Trentecoste and Brother Bobby R. Spears, have been there for our family without fail and have been unwavering pillars of strength for us during the tough times.

Thank you to all the medical personnel who contributed to the care of my family. Dr. Jerri Morrison was such a comfort and so empathetic to our suffering; her mother passed away from Muscular Dystrophy. Nona Sutton, Mike's hospice nurse and Shannon Hartzog, the social worker with Community Hospice of McComb, Mississippi were so available for Mike's every need. They went way beyond the call of duty many times. Thanks to every person who uttered a prayer, bought a CD, or helped in any manner.

Personal acknowledgements go to my book buddy, Larry Henderson Sr., who convinced me that my story was worth telling and worked tirelessly to help design my book cover and edit my manuscript. After reading my manuscript, Larry told me, "You need a rainbow ending." I thought about it and I realized I could indeed write a rainbow ending. I attribute the last chapter of my book to one of the most intelligent guys I have the privilege to know.

My daughter, Melissa, who encouraged me to start a journal several years ago, has been a constant source of strength through the many losses that just kept coming. Melissa displayed such strength during our painful times when I know her heart was broken. She is my leaning post. Thanks to Baron, my son-in-law, who took me into his home after my husband's death and showed such love and compassion.

vi

A special acknowledgement goes to my granddaughter, Whitney. The first chapter of this book was written from her incredibly vivid memory of the night that changed all of our lives. She was there, and even though she was only eight years old, the events were seared into her young mind. The years have passed, but the events of November 15 still brings raw emotion. Whitney was so hands on in the care of her dad. She adored him and did everything she could to bring a smile to his face. Whitney's help was invaluable in editing my work.

Thanks to all who read my book prior to publication and made me feel it would impart faith and encouragement to those who are suffering. Sue Fountain, Shelia Hall, Evie McNeese, Wayne Grant, Larry and Ann Henderson, Nancy Schlumbrecht, Rev. James Carney, Libby Magee, Rev. Carl Freeman, Melissa Desmond, Joy Stinson and BB Baynham, Whitney Smith, Joel Hill; thank you for your feedback.

Statements

"I love your story just the way it is.... Heart wrenching and inspiring. I fought tears until I finished it, then I bawled. Your bravery through Christ is amazing. Love you Sister Ann!"

Maresa Joy Stinson
Author of *Out of the Darkness*

"Barbara (Ann) Smith Hill is a living example of understanding and realizing, by her own experiences, God's mercies are new every day, and they are freely available to all of us. Barbara speaks out of experience and this book is a must-read for those who question God's love and care because of the painful things that have happened in life..... God Moment Miracles is not about providing answers but rather experiencing a heartfelt relational connection to both God and humanity during life's darkest hours."

Rev. James E. Carney

"Ann, I was one of the ones lucky enough to read your manuscript!! Not only was it written from the heart, it will bring awareness of this horrible disease to the attention of people like me that had no idea just how horrible MD is!! It brought me the ability to increase my faith as I read how God came on the scene in your life. Thank you so much for sharing your valleys and mountains with us. I can't wait to buy a copy!!! Love you!

Evie McNeese

"Upon reading this inspirational book, I was reminded of the goodness and faithfulness of God. As Ann's daughter, many of these stories are vivid memories from my past… This book brought me to the realization that we aren't going through trials alone. Not only do we have God with us, but at the same time, there are probably hundreds of people going through the same situation, or possibly something very similar…. I believe this book is beneficial for anyone… May God bless you as you read this book and enlighten you to His will for your life!"

Melissa Desmond

"Well, I've just finished reading your book. What can I say? It is wonderful, so inspiring, so touching and I had to stop and wipe the tears out of my eyes several times before I could continue. Barbara, only God could give you the strength to face the trials that you have endured. You go for it because I'm sure it will be a blessing to many that read it. You are a special person and your hardships in life have let you know that there is a God that loves us and is always there for us. I say get it to the publisher as soon as you can. Love you, Girl!"

Libby

"Ann, thank you for allowing me to read your manuscript of *God Moment Miracles* subtitled: *Blessings Disguised as Hardship*. I was drawn into your life, sharing your struggles and victories. The trip down memory lane of your life dealing with losses of your husband and children to this deadly disease was both emotional and personal. The book is energizing and gives positive encouragement for dealing with life's complications. Thank you for sharing."

Larry Henderson, Sr.
Author of *Ordinary Miracles: Science & Creation*

"Muscular Dystrophy is a very debilitating disease that not only affects the body of the person who has it, it also affects the family greatly. It's very difficult for the family watching their loved one slowly lose the ability to do for themselves. When that person is such a God fearing person they can be an inspiration to everyone around them."

Nona Sutton

(Mike's Hospice nurse)

God has blessed me to unimaginable lengths through Myotonic Muscular Dystrophy. I'm sure that sounds crazy, but God has worked in our lives in many miraculous ways over the years. This book, *God Moment Miracles*, displays these works in an awesome way. I hope that through this book, you are inspired by my family's struggles – and ultimately our miracles. Through the sickness of my amazing father, Mike, I learned how to overcome, persevere and what faith and trust in God <u>truly</u> is. This book is a great illustration that no matter how bad things may seem, God's plan is always true and He is the creator of the most beautiful rainbows!

Whitney Smith

Articles

REACHING OUT

MDAASAG NEWSLETTER

| Volume 2 Issue 10 | June 2008 | Gvdoman@yahoo.com |

IN MEMORY OF
MICHAEL LARRY SMITH
1965-2008

Michael was diagnosed with Myotonic Muscular Dystrophy in 1998 at 33 years of age while recovering from injuries sustained in an automobile accident. He was the first in his family to be diagnosed and because the disease is hereditary, it led to the diagnosis of his father, brothers, and two cousins. Michael's injuries accelerated the progression of the disease over the course of nine years resulting in respiratory complications that required a tracheostomy and mechanical ventilation while sleeping.

Michael spent four years in hospice defying all medical prognoses concerning life expectancy even while facing continuous medically documented decline and muscle deterioration. His doctors always admired his courage and tenacity while facing this devastating disease and frequently labeled him a medical miracle. His family is sure that medical textbooks would be written or enhanced with the addition of his medical situation as his disease progression was very unusual for MMD patients and in some areas, closely resembled Lou Gherig's disease (ALS). Michael lived like he died – with courage and tenacity – determined to squeeze in every ounce of life he could.

The devastation of this disease upon Michael's family brought them closer together and encouraged them to get involved in the Muscular Dystrophy Association's fundraising efforts by coordinating Shamrocks programs and assisting with the local MDA telethon. At his funeral, the family requested that instead of flowers, memorials be made in Michael's memory to several charitable organizations, including the Muscular Dystrophy Association. His wife, Shelia, has written and self-published a book entitled *Standing...Even on a Banana Peel: Encouragement for Caregivers of the Terminally Ill*, based upon her caregiving experiences while caring for Michael, a MMD patient.

Michael departed this life on January 26, 2008 at 42 years of age. He leaves to cherish his memory his wife Shelia and two children, Whitney and Michael Ray; his mother and step-father Ann and Joel Hill.

Stepping up

Nona Sutton goes above and beyond for families

BY ALLYSON REYNOLDS DIXON
ENTERPRISE-JOURNAL

Nona Sutton's job as a hospice nurse may have a lot to do with death and dying, but for at least one family her work was all about living life to its fullest.

In January 2005, Sutton began working with Mike and Sheila Smith's family in Brookhaven.

Sutton was the on-call nurse for Community Hospice of America (CHA) and came into contact with the family briefly. But her homeside manner was so special, that they requested her as their regular nurse.

Sutton went above and beyond, says Sheila Smith, widow of Mike Smith, who died in January.

After Hurricane Katrina, the family was displaced, and Smith visited them regularly at the special needs shelter.

"She promised us that as soon as she received power at her home, she would come and get us from the shelter to stay with her as long as necessary," Sheila Smith wrote in her nomination letter.

"Within one week of the hurricane, she obtained power and transferred our entire family to her home, where we stayed for the next 10 days. ... Nona did not have to do this as part of her job, nor was it expected. She just knew it needed to be done and did it."

Later, in 2007, Sheila's husband expressed a desire to go to the Super Bowl to meet all of the Mannings.

While that was impossible, Sutton and the CHA volunteer coordinator managed to get him a football signed by Archie Manning and autographed photos of Eli and Peyton Manning.

"It happened because Nona had such a compassionate heart and wanted to make one of his wishes come true," Sheila Sutton has been ...

SUBMITTED

Nona Sutton, left, holds up autographed memorabilia from Archie Manning and sons Peyton and Eli with the late Mike Smith.

> 'It happened because Nona had such a compassionate heart and wanted to make one of his last wishes come true.'
>
> **Sheila Smith**
> In nomination letter

1976, and in 1988, she started in home health.

She began her R.N. training a year later and has been with Community Hospice of America

Over the years, Sutton says, she has met many special families.

"I think most any nurse you talk to, there's attachments that are easily made," she says. "There's no way you can be a loving person and care for people and not get somewhat attached."

And many, Smith believes, grow attached to Sutton. Her family certainly did, and she feels Sutton is an unsung hero because her compassion is tempered with humility.

Those two qualities are what make her such a good nurse, Smith said.

"She's that type all the time," Smith says of Sutton. "Really, I want people who might think they don't want hospice to find out that it's good. But I also want to recognize Nona. She's very

xiii

MDA RESEARCH UPDATE ON MYOTONIC DYSTROPHY – YOUR DOLLARS MAKE A DIFFERENCE:

We thank Sharon Hesterlee, Phd., MDA Director of Research Development for sharing with the MDAASG some of the current MMD research. Dr. Hesterlee has concisely written for us where research has been, is and the realistic hope for the future.

MDA Research Update on Myotonic Dystrophy: Your Dollars Make A Difference

Myotonic muscular dystrophy, despite being the most common adult form of muscular dystrophy in the U.S., has remained largely a mystery until recently. The disease has many complex factors including a variety of symptoms, increasing severity through generations, and genetic defects that do not seem to directly cause all of the symptoms of the disease.

In the last few years, largely through research projects supported by MDA, the pieces of this puzzle have started to fall into place and the development of a therapy for this devastating disease has become realistic possibility. The following MDA-funded projects have contributed greatly to our understanding of this disease:

Second Genetic Defect For Myotonic Dystrophy Identified

Since 1992, when a genetic flaw on chromosome 19 was found to underlie most cases of myotonic dystrophy (MMD), there have been patients whose genetic test for the disease was negative but who appeared to have the disorder — puzzling scientists and families alike.

Now, MDA-sponsored investigators Laura Ranum and John Day of the Institute of Human Genetics at the University of Minnesota in Minneapolis appear to have at least partially solved the mystery. Ranum is a molecular biologist, and Day is a neurologist who directs the MDA clinic at Fairview University Medical Center.

In 1998, Ranum and Day found that there's a second form of MMD for which a defect is located on chromosome 3. In the Aug. 3 issue of the prestigious journal Science, the team announced that the flaw for this form of MMD is located inside a specific gene on chromosome 3 and that it consists of an expanded, repeated section of DNA.

Based on this discovery, Athena Diagnostics has already developed a genetic test for the second form of MMD (called DM2, as opposed to DM1 for the chromosome 19 form), which may lead to a definite genetic diagnosis for the forty percent of those with MMD symptoms who test negative for the better known form of the disease. It's also likely that the new findings will shed light on the causes of both disorders — a step that may ultimately lead to treatment.

Foreword

As my mind hurls backward through the years, I stand in awe of the miracles and supernatural resources that have come my way. There have been many God Moments that defy explanation. I know it is faith in an unfailing God that has caused me to triumph over mountains of sickness that has plagued my family. I am writing about these things to help someone who might be suffering from a loss, or going through a tragic experience. So many Christians give up on God when things go wrong in their lives. They feel there is no hope and no way out of a deep pit of depression which haunts them. I have been there and this book is dedicated to all who are in the mist of that battle. We do not lean on our own understanding, but learn to lean on a higher power.

My story is about the constant struggles that ensue when you suddenly learn three of your four children and your spouse have a genetic disease that threatens their life and guarantees death is stalking. The disease of Myotonic Muscular Dystrophy was unheard of in my life and I am sure many of you are only vaguely familiar with this dreaded disease. Until it hits our family or someone close to us, we take health and life for granted.

I was no different than most other people who felt compassion when I would see someone in a wheelchair or witness someone struggling to walk. I would briefly wonder in my mind what happened and why a young, beautiful person has to be confined to a wheelchair. I was vaguely familiar with the huge telethon held yearly on labor-day weekend. The term "Jerry's Kids" is well known to many. I regret I did not take the time to get to know the cause behind the incredible sacrifice by so many to help the cause of Muscular Dystrophy.

Myotonic Muscular Dystrophy is a neuromuscular disease that is genetic. It is only one type of many different types of Muscular Dystrophy. One of the more common types is ALS, also known as Lou Gehrig. Usually with ALS, your life expectancy is up to five years from the time of diagnosis. Steinert is the technical medical term for Myotonic Muscular Dystrophy and the expected life span with Myotonic Muscular Dystrophy is greater than most of the other types. Some of the other types of dystrophy are; Becker (BMD), Acid Maltese (AM) Amyotrophic Lateral Sclerosis (ALS) Duchenne (DMD), Emery Driefuss (EDMD), Limb-Girdle (LGMD), and Myosthenia Gravis (MG).

These are very debilitating diseases and from time of diagnosis, there is no expected improvement. The disease only gets worse with time and eventually will claim your life. MMD affects a person by contracting the muscles, but not allowing them to relax. The muscles also grow steadily weaker. This can be devastating with the heart muscle as well as the pleura around the lungs. Basically, this disease affects every part of the body. The eyes are usually affected by cataracts at a very young age. In the advanced stage, most hearing is lost. Every muscle in the body cannot function properly. It affects swallowing, speech and the body's mobility.

I have personally dealt with one of these neuromuscular diseases through my husband and children. I have lost my husband and two of my four children. I have a son that suffers daily; he too is terminally ill. The challenges come like the waves of an ocean, just as you rise above one, another hits you. This story is the journey of our family's experience with Myotonic Muscular Dystrophy. It is a story I pray will give you a sense of what it means to be an overcomer. Some of my darkest hours were spent watching my oldest son, Michael, struggle on a ventilator for more than nine years. He probably holds the Guinness World Record for Hospice care after receiving care for over five years.   Experiencing his courage, and recognizing God's Moments of Miracles has given me the ultimate picture of what true courage and faith really is.

**The Smith Children -- Back: Matthew, Mark
Front: Melissa, Mike**

Grands

Allysse

Whitney

Seth

Alissa

Erik

Michael

Mark Scott

Chapter 1

November 15

Sunday, November 15, 1998, began as any other cold and rainy November day. After church that evening, my oldest son, Michael, and his children were on their long drive home to Mississippi. In my heart, I knew something was amiss; my heart and mind were beyond troubled as I fell asleep.

Little did I know, at approximately the same time as I was falling asleep, my sweet son and his precious children were traveling down China Grove Road with its infamously dangerous s-curve. Whitney was in the front seat next to her father and Michael was in the back seat lying down, fast asleep.

Upon reaching this well-known s-curve, one small moment caused our family's entire future to be altered as God knew it would be. Mike fell asleep at the wheel, causing him to hit the standing water on the road from the day's rough rains and hydroplane. After hitting the water, Mike lost control of the car completely due to a lack of grip on the steering wheel; he could not keep the car in line after hitting that water. The vehicle spun around four complete times in the middle of the curve, flipped over three times to ultimately land in the ditch with the passenger side down on the opposite side of the road than they were driving.

Mike, Whitney and Michael were not wearing seatbelts; so it was incredible they did not get killed! With the passenger side of the car being down toward the ground and Mike not having a seatbelt on, he was having to constantly hold himself up so he would not fall down on top of Whitney in the car. There are no homes on that particular stretch of road in that large curve and the ditch they landed in was so deep that you could barely see the tops of the wheels on the car. A passerby would not notice unless they happened to be looking at the ditch as they passed. It was a short stretch of time with cars passing before someone saw the wheels of the car and went to call an ambulance and the police. When the paramedics and police arrived, they had to remove the back windshield to get Michael out of the car. He was the easiest to remove from the vehicle.

Whitney and Mike were not as easy to get out of the car. Whitney was closest to the ground in the car, and Mike still had to consciously and consistently hold himself up to keep her from getting crushed from his weight. The police and firemen were not able to get the front windshield off the car since the frame had been crushed in from flipping over three times. There was no space left there for them to get Whitney out of the car. The roof of the car was also smashed in a good bit, so the space in the vehicle between the roof and the seats was reduced dramatically.

Eventually, they were able to wiggle Whitney through the gap between the driver and passenger seats. They had to get Mike lifted up for that gap between the seats to be available: his grip was slipping from holding himself up for so long when he was seriously injured. Only the love of a parent when knowing their child will be hurt can accomplish what seems impossible. The paramedics, police and firemen knew they had to hurry to get Whitney out of the car. They managed to get Mike lifted up for a moment, Whitney through the seats and out of the back windshield area of the car. As soon as Mike knew Whitney was out of the car, he relinquished his grip at last and fell to the bottom of the car.

The next hurdle was getting Mike out of the car. Removing him through the front windshield was not an option. They could not get him through the gap in the seats to go out through the back due to his size and none of the doors could be opened because of the multiple flips. The jaws-of-life were their only option to get him out of the car. The paramedics could not see the extent of his injuries while he was still in the car, but they knew he was in incredible pain. He kept repeating,

"God, I hurt!" These exclamations made the paramedics even more frantic to get him out of the car.

They used the jaws-of-life, and after about an hour, he was on a stretcher headed to the hospital. Mike kept saying over and over, "God, I hurt!" These words were his plea to God; the only words he could utter while in such pain.

November 15, 1998 is a date that is forever etched in my memory. Since that horrific night, so many questions have arisen, so many trials have been conquered and my family has been blessed exponentially through the struggles. This book is my family's history, my family's story in the seemingly never-ending fight with Myotonic Muscular Dystrophy.

Chapter 2

Humble Beginnings: Faith and Heritage

The Mannings
Left to right: Yancy, Odie, Verna, Everett, Viola, Homer, Corine)

My story, like so many others, begins humbly. As a small child in a family of eight children, I can recall being very poor. I was the third child born on April 2, 1947 to my parents, Alvie Freeman and Odie Manning Freeman. It was not because of laziness that we were poor. There was no one who worked harder than my mother and my father was sick most of the time. My mother only had a third grade education, so any type of public work was out of the question. Regardless of her limitations, mom realized her dream. She asked God to help her children receive an education because she had been deprived of one. Even though she had very little financial help, she managed to see all eight of her children graduate from high school, and each obtained advanced career training and education, including one Master's degree.

More important than education, mother taught us the principles of Godly living. She taught us self-respect and determination. Her motto was, "Do unto others as you would have them do unto you." This philosophy was adopted from scripture found in Luke 6:31. She had such love and I know God had his hand on my mother's life. There were times when she did not know what would be our next meal. Matthew 6:34 tells us to "take no thought for tomorrow" about what we are to wear or what we have to eat. My mother's life exemplified that scripture; her faith was astounding.

There were times when someone would bring us money or groceries that only God could have let them know our need. Even after I was grown and lived in a different state than my mother, I would always ask her about food and ask if she needed anything. Her reply would always be, "I'll be alright. Don't you worry about me, I'm fine." Sometimes I would get in my car and drive to check on her after hanging up the phone.

When I would walk in and look around, her cupboard would be bare, there would be very little in the refrigerator and her last meal would be on the stove. "I thought you told me you were fine. You do not have any food. Why didn't you tell me?" I would say.

In April 2013 God called my brother home after he suffered a massive stroke. He was an inspiration to all who knew him.

One afternoon, when I was around the age of eight years old, we were in the field picking cotton. Doing field work was how we survived. We heard mom's voice boom out, "Run! Run for the house! There is a storm coming!" We knew by the tone of her voice we needed to go. We ran, and barely made it inside before the wind and rain began to blow. Mom told us to get in the second room and kneel around the bed and pray.

We could hear the wind howling violently outside. We became very scared as we heard the sounds of a violent storm and felt so helpless. We had hardly begun to pray, when it was all over. The wind subsided and as we looked outside; there was destruction everywhere! The front room of our little three room house was gone. A huge oak tree that was right in front of our house was twisted like a match stick and was lying across the road. What a close call we had! A tornado had roared through and left a path of destruction.

I will always believe because we were kneeling and praying in that second room, God spared our lives. What if the big oak tree had fallen the opposite way? We would have all been crushed! The whole structure of that little house would have collapsed. When you are in the storm whether in life or literally, prayer changes things! It can mean the difference between life and death, spiritually or physically.

A year later, in the summer of 1957, is another time in my youth I remember very vividly. We were picking cotton at my aunt Corine's house. It was nearing the end of the day and I remember being very tired. Suddenly, I felt a sharp prick on my foot and as I looked down, I noticed two little specks of blood on the side of my foot. We went barefoot most of the time because shoes were kept for school or special occasions. Thinking I had stepped on a cotton burr, I did not bother to call anyone or bring any attention to myself. After a few moments, I began to feel sleepy and still not comprehending the gravity of my situation, I laid down and went to sleep in the middle of the cotton row.

Some time had passed before my first cousin, Hubert, found me. My foot was swollen terribly and he knew something was wrong. He called to my mom and everyone came running. There was a debate about what might be wrong. After noticing the marks on my foot, the tentative conclusion was that I had probably been bitten by a snake. Rattlesnakes were abundant in this rural area in Mississippi. My Uncle's dog had been bitten a week or two earlier and had died.

I was rushed to the emergency room, which was around fifteen miles away and was kept in the emergency room for quite a while. Due to the part of the south we were in, it was determined I probably had been bitten by a rattlesnake. After enduring a nine day hospital stay, and coming very close to losing my life, I pulled through this very traumatic event. I remember how my leg took on a remarkable likeness of a snake, which seemed very strange to me as a child. It took several months for this to disappear. Most people have a natural fear of snakes but this event sealed a lasting impression upon me to steer clear of those slithering reptiles, whether they are poisonous or not.

I was very demanding, not wanting mom to leave me alone. At the age of nine, I did not understand the demands of being a parent, especially one with seven other children to consider. Being the third child, there were five who were younger than me. Mom had to be incredibly tired. I do not see how she managed, because we had no means of transportation. Everywhere we went, we had to rely on someone else.

I greatly admire my mom because of the devoted and loving person she was. Mom loved children. Every child around found their way to our house because they were always made to feel welcome. We would share whatever food we had if company was present at mealtime. Mom made most of our clothes, at least for the four girls. She quilted, took in ironing, cleaned houses, and did anything she could to make money to provide for us. She was really amazing. She lived her life with dignity and grace, though at times I know she was broke and broken.

I do not have very many good memories of my dad. I know he was ill, but he was not home enough for us to realize we had a dad. Mom had to do it all, with nothing to rely on but her own abilities. She raised us to love and respect each other and to help each other in times of need. That lesson has been with us throughout our lives and is still evident today. Even though mom is gone, the love and kindness she exemplified has molded the character of all of her children. Bitterness and anger were not part of her beautiful character, even though she probably had more reason than most to be angry and bitter. She was twenty three when she married, then only after her last sister had married and gone. She felt such a responsibility toward her siblings. They regarded her as a mother more than a sister.

In October 1966, at the age of fifty-two, mom needed to have one of her kidneys removed. I remember this event so well because I had just become pregnant with my second child and was extremely sick most of the time. I was determined though, I was going to be with her during this very serious operation. Her kidney and urethra tube was scheduled to be removed. The incision was from the middle of her back all the way around to the middle of her stomach. At the time, there were no short cuts. Even gall bladder surgery was considered a dangerous surgery. Medical technology had made tremendous advances since then.

There was a young doctor who did his best to get me a lounge chair to sleep on, but not long after he brought it, security came and got it. I had it pretty rough. This happened at the Charity Hospital in New Orleans, Louisiana.

I was only twenty-two and had never been very far from the country roads of Louisiana, so this big hospital was pretty scary to me. As I was entering the elevator to go down, I glimpsed a man running to catch it. I was the only one inside and he barely made it before the doors closed. As he entered he was holding his stomach and I glanced away, trying not to acknowledge him. My eyes darted back to him and automatically went to his hand that was holding his stomach. To my horror blood was oozing through his fingers! I was petrified, to say the least! I did not know what happened and it seemed it was taking forever for the elevator to reach the first floor.

The doors opened and there stood two uniformed policemen who immediately grabbed him and took him away. I found out his wife worked on the floor I had come from and she shot him. I had never seen anyone shot before and do not want that experience again.

I regret my mom grew so used to not getting any of her own desires. She made crafted quilts, which took a lot of time as every stitch was done by hand, and I think this was very therapeutic for her. She was a quiet person and very seldom would you see any open emotion. She learned to be quiet and never complain very early in her life. I love her so much. I know she endured untold pain here on this earth, but she did not let it make her bitter. She had one of the sweetest spirits and she loved children with a special love. In her subconscious, she tried to protect any child who was threatened or hungry.

Mom told me about a little child at the bus stop in New Orleans, Louisiana, when she had to go to the doctor. She only had enough money to buy one hamburger and the trip to the doctor was an all-day affair since she had to travel by bus. As she was about to eat her lunch, a little boy was looking at her intently. Mom felt the child was hungry, so she forgot about her own hunger. She gave the child her hamburger. That was my mom. Everyone else's needs always came before her own.

As a child, you do not perceive or understand the grown up world. There were eight of us kids, as mom had one child after the other. Mom raised her six siblings and then married into a life that was even harder for her. You would think after years of hardship, marriage would be a welcome escape, but it did not turn out that way.

My dad would be home for short periods of time, then he would be in the hospital while my mom had to deal with the family, finances and survival. My dad suffered from mental illness. I remember a narrow escape once when dad chased mom with a knife. If my oldest brother had not intervened, who knows how that would have turned out? I was happier when dad was not around because it was more peaceful. That sounds unkind, but children are very impacted by conflict and drama within the home.

Mom was in her seventies when she was given the grim news she had bladder cancer. She battled this disease for several years until she lost the battle in 1992. I suspect this was the same thing that had claimed her mother at a much younger age.

The poem below came to me one day as I was heading to the hospital where she was undergoing another operation. She had taken all the radiation and chemotherapy she could. My mind was racing ahead and I wondered if this was the end. I thought of the life that she had lived, the hardships, the struggles.

A PORTRAIT OF MY MOM, ODIE

She worked and toiled her whole life through,
Scrimping and managing and just making do,
Washing, ironing and mending too,
I never heard her say, "I want",
Neither pride nor beauty did she flaunt.

Sacrifice is a word that she knew well,
Never a home of her own in which to dwell,
She was happy though, and this is why,
She knew how to give and not deny.

The simple things would bring her joy,
Feeding a little girl or a little boy,
Quilting her quilts, cooking a meal,
With the sweetest smile that was real.

Loving and caring for others,
She helped to raise her sisters and brothers,
Her mother passed on when she was young,
Into great responsibility she was flung.

Then she started a life of her own,
With eight more children to see full grown,
She prayed a lot for the Lord to make a way,
He did, from day to day.

Surely, Mom with a portrait like this,
Heaven has saved a place with all its bliss,
Just for you, so you'll know what it's like,
Not to worry or fret, or break up a fight.

The streets of gold and the river of life,
Flow gently by and there is no strife,
The angels sing and the heavens ring,
For my sweet mom, Odie, to bring,
A soul that's free and a voice to sing.

By Ann Smith Hill

Mother managed to pull through one more time, but the doctor sent her home to die. She did not know her time was so near. She kept thinking God was going to heal her and bring her back to health. My sister, Shelia, who was a nurse, took a leave of absence from her job to stay with her until the end. Shelia told me as mother was nearing the end, she became very restless.

She was so weak and was past speaking, so we had to try to figure out what to do for her. Mom read her Bible every day until she was no longer able to. We knew how much she loved and depended on her God.

On this particular night Shelia told me nothing seemed to work. She could not make mom comfortable no matter what she did. Shelia said she walked into the living room and found her Bible. She went back into the room and laid the Bible on the bed and began to pray. A sudden peace descended upon my mother and she rested the entire night. God is so good! He loves His children so much. If we could only know and realize He really cares.

The night my mom entered heaven is one I will always remember. As I left work that day and headed to see her, I was not there very long before I felt God was going to take her to glory. About midnight, Shelia convinced me to go home, saying she could last several days and since I had to work, there was no need to stay.

About four o'clock in the morning, the phone rang and I immediately knew she was gone. I hurried over and arrived before the coroner got there. I walked into the room and there lay my sweet and precious mother, still and peaceful as life had departed her frail body. There was such a look of peace upon her face. She was resting in the arms of a loving God. She had fought a good fight, kept the faith and her crown was waiting.

"So shalt thou find favour and good understanding in the sight of God and man."

Proverbs 3:4

Chapter 3

Growing Up

Barbara Ann Freeman
(Ann Smith Hill)
Prom 1964

My first job was at the age of twelve while I stayed with a nice couple and worked the summer. I felt very grown up having a job. That summer taught me many things as I began to venture into life away from my siblings. I learned to make the best snowball in the south and later in life I opened a snowball business of my own. My second job was babysitting. I was thirteen and became very good friends with Ann Thomas, a third grade teacher from the school I attended. She had two little boys who stole my heart.

After a fire and losing her home, my friend Ann, decided to move back to her mother's home in Bessemer, Alabama. I really missed her, and when she came back for a few days, she wanted to know if I would go spend a couple of weeks with her in Alabama. I was so excited. My sweet mother let me go but it was very hard for her. She trusted Ann.

As I arrived in Alabama, I walked into a new and very different world than I had ever experienced. Ann's mother was so elegant and her home was like a mansion to me. Of course, it was a middle class home, but at the time I felt like Cinderella going to the castle. This was the first time in my life I experienced a table adorned with a real tablecloth and actual place settings complete with dinnerware, glassware, and an array of silverware. I did not know anything about table etiquette. I had no idea what a salad fork was, or what a soup spoon was. I wondered what a knife was doing by the plate.

I learned so much that summer about so many things. I received an education I have taken with me throughout my life. I adore setting a beautiful table and using different and unusual table settings. I collect antique dishes and glassware and it all goes back to the summer I spent in Bessemer, Alabama. I would have to say, other than my mother, my friend, Ann, influenced my life more than anyone else. To me, Ann lived the perfect life. She was a drum majorette and knew how to play a piano so well I could sit and listen for hours. She was scheduled to become a concert pianist when she decided to get married. She had the awesome privilege of going to college.

I was supposed to visit for two weeks, but it turned

into the whole summer. I was having so much fun and learning so much about life, I did not want to go home. I had no idea how much my poor mother was suffering because one of her chicks was not in the nest. She knew I was okay but my mother missed me and wanted me home. My friend, Ann, did not realize how much mom missed me. My mother was frantic but she had no means to come and get me. I do not think we had a telephone at that time so the only means of communication was writing letters.

I finally came home after the summer was over. Needless to say, that would never happen again. I did come home with some nice clothes to start school, and I was entering high school, so I was a happy camper. Ann's sister and brother-in-law had no children and both of them had good jobs. They wanted mother to let me live with them to see that I got a college education. Herman was a professor at Mt. Berry College in Rome, Georgia and Betty was a lab technician. I must have touched their hearts because they were so good to me. Herman took me on a train ride that was a first for me. I saw what an education could do for you, so I wanted to pursue mine and live the way these people lived. I never knew this kind of life existed, except in books.

Years later I ran into Ann in a local hospital ICU waiting room. She lost her companion, Richard while we were there. I got to see those sweet little boys I had spent so much time with. They were all grown up and had their own families. One of the boys looked like Richard Gere. He was a very handsome young man. It was a bittersweet moment, knowing the reason they were there. Ann had recently moved back to

Franklinton, Louisiana.

I was a cheerleader in high school and loved it. I loved going to the games and dancing around in my short little skirt, living in a different world with my dreams. In 2010 I attended a class reunion and one of my classmates, whom I had always been close to, told me she had wanted to be as pretty as I was.

I was a bright student, earning mostly A's and a few B's. I loved learning. In my junior year, I was chosen to present the Key to the senior class which was a yearly ritual. Someone from the junior class would make a speech and present the Key to a chosen senior. I was so honored to get this privilege. I had met the star basketball player, Larry Smith and we were dating regularly. He was an awesome person and incredibly good looking.

I wanted to look amazing for the Junior-Senior Banquet that was held each year. Today it is called prom. Mom took me to buy my dress for the special occasion. We looked and looked and I could not seem to find the perfect dress. Finally, mom said, "The only place left to try is Rosenblum's." I knew it was the most expensive department store in town. I also knew we could not afford a dress from this store. We went in and there was the perfect dress. I had never seen a dress I thought was more beautiful. Mom looked at the price tag and told the sales lady we would come back to purchase it. I thought that was just a way to leave the store. I knew we did not have the money to buy it. Oh well, I would do something. My disappointment was visible I'm sure, but mom said we would get it some way. I tried to forget about the dress, and tried not to show my feelings because I knew she was doing the best she could.

The day came for the banquet and I still did not have a dress. I was thinking I would have to stay home. Mom had gone to town that day and when she returned, she called me to come and see something. I felt sure she had managed to buy me a dress of some kind, and I was determined I was going to act excited no matter what the dress looked like. To my utter amazement, when she opened the bag, out came the beautiful dress I wanted so badly. How in the world did she do it? I was so happy I was beside myself. I forgot about how she did it; I just reveled in the fact I was going to look amazing at the banquet. I still do not know how my sweet mother got the dress.

"Not by works of righteousness which we have done, but according to His mercy He saved us, by the washing of regeneration, and renewing of the Holy Ghost."

Titus 3:5

Chapter 4

The Journey

     I continued dating Larry throughout high school and on October 24, 1964 we were married in a small but beautiful home ceremony. We were very young, ages seventeen and eighteen. Larry won a scholarship to play basketball at Southwest Mississippi Community College. We lived with his parents and he commuted twenty miles to school, but in his second year we lived on the college campus in an apartment for married couples.

Soon we were blessed with our first child. I will never forget how my husband stood over me and thanked me for his beautiful son. We named our firstborn Michael Larry, after his Dad. Michael was a very beautiful child and brought much joy to the Smith household. This was a very special time in our life when I felt so much love and happiness.

Because I was so young, my mother-in law came to my rescue many times. She taught me so much about caring for and handling a small child. We took Michael to basketball games and followed Larry wherever he was playing. Larry was a very good player and put his heart into every game. We were so proud of his trophy at the end of the basketball season.

I worked at a local hospital as a switchboard operator while my husband attended college. After Larry completed college, he took a job with Firestone Tire Company and I went to work as a bookkeeper for a sand and gravel business.

One of my first God Moments came when my oldest child, Michael, was nine months old. He started out with the normal cold, but it soon progressed to pneumonia in both lungs and a fever of 105 degrees. He was admitted to the local hospital which was a small hospital and by today's standards, very primitive. The hospital consisted of three doctors, all brothers; and a small nursing staff. They packed my little fellow in ice to try to bring his fever down. This is a practice that is not done anymore.

He was given strong antibiotics and began to respond. After a few days in the hospital, he was discharged. We took him home and severe diarrhea started due to the strong medicine. We had to readmit him to the hospital and due to my work schedule we relied on my mother-in-law to help at the hospital. Because of our youth and never having dealt with a sick child, we did not realize the gravity of the situation. Mike was dehydrated and very sick. He was already weak from the bout with pneumonia. We had no idea another sickness was inside his young and frail body. This bout with pneumonia and diarrhea happened at such a young age and the pneumonia had an impact on his lungs for the rest of his life.

A nurse came in and was trying to administer medicine to him when he choked. The nurse panicked and gave Michael to my mother-in-law and ran out of the room to get help. Mom was left with a choking child. The only thing she knew to do was pray. I was at work and oblivious to the dire situation until later when I arrived at the hospital.

Mom was still visibly shaken at what had occurred. We really came close to losing our nine month old son. Thank you, God, for allowing a Godly, praying woman to be with our little one when a miracle was needed. I was not in the church at the time, so Mom being with Michael at this particular moment was divinely ordered. Over the course of Michael's life, there were so many things that was inspirational to all who had the privilege to know him. Michael slowly got well and grew normally after that.

Soon we had another bundle of joy in our home. Our second son was named Marcus Lamar. Mark was a little premature and weighed five pounds and fourteen ounces. He had medical problems from the time he was born. It seemed Mark cried all the time. He was so small and we were constantly at the doctor's office.

When Mike was two years old, we had another incident that was extremely scary. Our second son, Mark, was only a few months old and I was working from home keeping books. One morning, I allowed Michael to go into the yard to play. I always kept my eye on him. He would usually stay in a certain little play area he liked.

On this particular morning, I was changing Mark's diaper when the phone rang. We did not have cordless or cell phones so I was at the desk. The phone call lasted a couple of minutes. As soon as I hung up the phone, I dashed outside to make sure Mike was still in his play area. He wasn't! I called him but received no answer. I thought, "He can't be far!" I went all the way around the house calling him. He was nowhere in sight, and panic began to overtake me. I know he did not just disappear! There was no traffic due to the fact we lived on a little lane and the highway was too far away. He had to be here. After a few more minutes, true terror was beginning to well up inside me.

I called Larry and told him I could not find Michael. He said, "What do you mean, you can't find him?" I started crying; He could tell I was panic stricken. He said he would be right there. It was about a ten minute drive into town and he was home within five.

As he got out of the car, his questions began to bombard me, "Where did you last see him?" I went over everything I could recall and we both were looking every place we could think to look. "We have to call the police, we need some help" Larry said, because our efforts were proving fruitless. We were in a state of panic. By this time about thirty minutes had passed. We called the police and Mom and Dad, who lived twenty miles away. It was another thirty minutes before they arrived.

The police arrived in record time and the questions started again. I know they were doing their job but by this time I was beginning to think something awful had happened. I could not think straight any more. I was beginning to lose it. The policeman told me it was very important that I pull myself together so I could help them. Mom and Dad arrived and all I could do was cry. They were frantic. I had a small child to take care of, so I would go from outside searching to inside.

Larry asked me if I had seen the dog. I had completely forgotten about the small white dog we had recently acquired. The dog never entered my mind. I remember thinking, "What's the dog got to do with this?" The police had broadened their search to near the highway. I remember saying, "He did not go to the highway." By this time over an hour had gone by. For a two-year old to be out of sight for this long was not good. Every possibility was crossing my mind. How could he disappear?

Then I heard the words I will forever be grateful for: "Here he is!" The sound was coming from the highway.   One of the officers saw him as he was emerging from the edge of the woods, across the highway. He was following the little white dog that had wandered off. This could have ended so differently.   I will always believe my praying mother-in-law touched the throne for my child---again!

When Mark was three years old, he began to lose his hair.   He was getting bald spots and we knew something was wrong. After a specialist examined him, the only thing the doctor could figure out was that Mark's body was not absorbing protein. The doctor recommended we take him off all foods with protein and gradually add them back to his diet to see if his body would respond. He gradually improved, but was always very small and his hair never grew normally. I wish we could have received the correct diagnosis at that time. It might have helped us with circumstances later, but research and diagnosis were not readily available at the time. Many people passed away without their families ever knowing what really caused them to die.

One day, my sweet mother-in-law invited me to go to church with her. The church mom attended was in revival and mostly out of respect for her, I went. Church was not a part of my life at the time. I had felt God calling me several years earlier, but I had pushed the thought of God away and went on with my life. As I entered this little country church, I did not know my life would be forever changed. I felt God's call in my life again, just as forceful as I felt it long ago, sitting on a different pew. I answered God's call in my life and his grace has sustained me through many years.

I began to study the Bible because I wanted to

know and do what was right and pleasing to God. The more I read, the clearer everything was to me. I loved to hear the Word of God and I still do. God's word was so special and I drank from the Word with a very thirsty soul! My experience with salvation has changed my life completely. I do not think the same or act the same. I am a new creature in Christ Jesus. If you see someone and they tell you they are saved, ask them if they are a new creature. If they have not changed, then I would question if they have really found God.

By this time, Larry and I had our third child, Matthew Lee. The same doctor, Dr. Walter Crawford, delivered all of our children. He was not a gynecologist, but we trusted him. Matthew was a beautiful baby boy with blue eyes and blond hair. We did not have the problems with Matthew when he was small that we encountered with Marcus. Thankfully, Matthew grew normally and had few medical problems. With three small children, one being sick was plenty. I do not know what I would have done if they would have all had problems early in life. God allowed them to have a pretty normal childhood. We had the usual bike wrecks, go cart mishaps, scrapes and bruises from varying incidents, but overall, pretty normal.

One of the silliest things I can remember doing was giving my five and six year old boys BB guns for Christmas. Whatever was I thinking? The only excuse I have is I did not realize what I was doing. Not long after they received these guns, I heard a scream and ran to see what was wrong. As I rushed into the room, there stood Mark screaming in pain. I immediately saw a small dark red dot in the middle of his forehead with blood oozing from it. Oh, no! I examined the small hole and could not determine if there was a BB in his head, so I put him in the car and headed toward the hospital.

About half way there, I decided to pull over and examine the wound a little more closely. I made the determination the BB had not lodged in his head and it was just a surface wound, so I turned around and headed back home. Needless to say, I took those guns and was incredibly thankful the aim was not a little lower to the right or left. He would have lost one of his eyes had that been the case. I still shake my head in disbelief that I actually gave my kids BB guns at that age.

With three small children (especially boys) and working, there are mishaps that escape your knowledge at the time they occur. One day when Matt was about three, I was bathing him and felt a soft spot on the top of his head. The more I examined it, the more alarmed I became. I began to question him about what he had done and how he had received some kind of blow to his head. He finally told me he had been playing with a brick and it hit him in the head. We rushed him to the emergency room, because it was apparent there was bleeding under the scalp. I did not know what else might be going on. After his examination and x-rays, it was determined that no fractures had occurred. He just had some bleeding under his scalp. The doctor drew the excess blood off and sent us home, telling us that if it became puffy again, to bring him back and he would draw off the excess blood.

Chapter 5

An Ever Present Help

When Mark was five years old, another major incident occurred in his life that I can say was indeed a divine God Moment Miracle. Mark was always very small and sickly. In the early seventies, if a child was small and sickly, it seemed the first thing a doctor did was recommend the child's tonsils be removed. Mark was scheduled for a tonsillectomy on a Friday, so we checked into the hospital on Thursday afternoon. He was NPO (nothing by mouth) after midnight and he had his surgery on schedule the next morning.

Soon after arriving back in his room after surgery, he started hemorrhaging and was rushed back into surgery. He was brought back to the room and discharged later that same afternoon. The next afternoon, Mark started vomiting; he had not eaten any food since Thursday before he entered the hospital. I was very concerned. I called the doctor who treated him at the hospital and was told it was not unusual for him to react in this manner. By Sunday morning I was frantic because he seemed to be getting steadily worse. Larry and I decided we needed to take him to the emergency room.

We drove to the small local hospital and one of the three doctors who owned the hospital was there to treat him. The doctor reeked of alcohol and gave our very sick son a shot for nausea and sent us home. On our way home, I told my husband if we did not do something, Mark was going to die. We immediately turned the car around and headed to McComb, Mississippi where he had been discharged from having his tonsillectomy.

Our small and frail child was extremely sick. Something had to be done, and quickly. When he was evaluated by the doctor, he was dehydrated and immediately treated with IV fluids. He was admitted to the hospital, but by this time he was so weak he seemed almost lifeless. He was breathing, but I was so scared. The doctor came by the room and gave us the grim news that the blood work indicated Mark was possibly suffering from appendicitis and would probably have to go back to surgery. The doctor informed us he was going to wait until the next morning, hoping the attack would subside. Early that Monday morning, the doctor came in and said, "I really do not want to operate on him, but I have no choice. He is not getting better." With those words, he left the room.

Several family members were there and someone had called our sweet pastor, Brother Earl Carney. I went to the side of the bed and began to pray. I had not been a Christian very long, but prayer was a huge part of our Christian faith. I was oblivious to everyone in the room as I sought God for help. Larry, Mom and I were bombarding heaven for intervention for this very sick child. The surgery team came into the room while we were praying and quietly waited until we finished. As they took our son out of the room a peace descended upon me that could only come from God. I felt our son was going to be okay. He was not in surgery very long, as an appendectomy is not usually considered a dangerous surgery. If I had known then about the underlying disease in his little body, I would have been even more concerned.

After surgery, Mark was incredibly weak, but I know God gave me a miracle that day. When he left the hospital, at five years old, he only weighed twenty one pounds. He looked like a little skeleton. If the doctor had known muscular dystrophy was in his young body, he would have been more concerned than he already was. Many years passed before we knew what had created problems throughout his life.

When our boys were ages six, four and two we bought a mobile home. Larry was now going to church with me, and I was very thankful. Since being called to the beautiful life of being a Christian, I had been praying diligently for my husband to join me. His mom was one of the sweetest and kindest people I have ever known. I loved my mother-in-law for many reasons. The love in her heart was evident to all. She brought me to God, not just by inviting me to church, but by the beautiful, loving spirit she displayed on a daily basis. She was a true Christian.

We were about two weeks into a six week revival. We went to church every night, seven nights a week. I worked at a small town manufacturing plant called Rutter Rex in Franklinton, Louisiana, which was about twenty miles from where we lived. I had to get up at five in the morning to be on my job for seven. I would get our three small boys up, dress them, drop them off at a local day care or my mother-in-law's and leave for work. We would get off at four and I would go home to pick up the boys, cook supper, get ready and head to church. The thing that stands out in my mind is that I did not get tired. I was so excited about my new found religion and love for the gospel, church was not a dread or boring. I could not wait to get there.

On this particular night, I had rushed home, cooked, bathed the kids, and busied myself getting ready for our usual church night. Larry came in and evidently had a very stressful day, because he said, "I believe I will stay here and watch the kids tonight."

I thought for a moment and replied, "Oh, honey, please come and let's all go. You will be blessed a lot more if you go". He reluctantly agreed and we all piled into the car and went to church.

We were at the end of the service and I was at the altar praying with someone who was seeking God. I noticed some commotion at the back of the church, but had no idea what was happening. I had trained myself to ignore distractions when someone was praying. Someone came up to me and called me aside. I do not remember who told me the grim news, but someone said, "Sister Ann, your trailer just burned. Brother Larry has gone with some of the men to see what happened."

I was on the second day of a three day fast. God had prepared me for this. I was in shock for a short period of time, but as I brought my mind to dwell on what had happened, I began to give thanks to God. Some probably thought I had lost my mind, but all I could think of was how close my children and husband had come to staying home.

It was determined the fire started in the kitchen, which was in the middle of the trailer. The children's rooms were on one end and our bedroom was on the other end. It was a real possibility that Larry would not have been able to reach the children. There was no way to escape from the children's rooms, so I was grateful I had my children and husband. We lost everything. Thank you, God, for one more time You kept us safe and let no harm come to us physically.

The generosity displayed by our church family as they reached out to help us during this tragic event was amazing. The Tupelo Children's Mansion in Tupelo, Mississippi sent my boys a lot of clothing. These children needed things themselves and were concerned about others. I will always remember these children for reaching out and wanting to help someone else. We invited some of these children to come during the summer and stay with us. We have contact with one of the mansion boys who lives in Oklahoma and has his own family. My daughter Melissa and her husband Baron regularly support the Tupelo Children's Mansion.

We lost some things that were not replaceable. One of these was my mother-in-law's treasured Bible that she had owned for a long time. I borrowed it to study from since it was old and contained some things in it the newer Bibles did not have. She was heartbroken over the Bible, but she did her best to hide her disappointment. Many years later, I was visiting Mom's first cousin and noticed that she had a Bible like the one that burned. I asked if she would consider selling it and she refused. She gave it to me. I was elated and very excited to find such a treasure. I could not wait to take it to Mom. She wanted to know where I had found it. I told her the Lord had provided. We were both extremely happy.

Another prized possession we lost in the fire was some 16x20 pictures of our three boys. I treasured these pictures because we were not able to afford professional portraits very often. I tried to track down the company to get reprints, but that effort was unsuccessful. Most of the things we accumulated through time could be replaced, but there were some things that proved to be irreplaceable. Someone had given my husband some old silver dollars for graduation from high school. We had protected those precious coins, not because of their monetary value as much as the sentimental value. Most of these were lost in the fire, but we did manage to find a few in the rubble.

After we lost our mobile home, we moved into a house owned by a good friend of ours, Charles. He was our pastor's son. God always provides! Matthew was three years old and I remember him learning to ride a bike while we lived next door to Charles and Nelda. He was determined to ride the bike without training wheels, so we took them off. He rode it, but he was so tired from all the exertion that he laid his bike down and I found him sound asleep in a ditch by our house. The bike was lying across him. At first I thought he had a wreck and was injured. Upon further inspection, I found he was sound asleep. He had gone as far as he could go!

Matthew was quite the explorer. He was a very curious child and could get into some situations. Once he climbed a tree in our front yard. He was still only three years old. He managed to get almost to the top of the tree without any thought of how he was going to get down. I was inside the house and had no idea what his latest adventure was. My brother Don was visiting and happened to walk by as he heard, "Help me! Help me!" coming from the top of the tree. I think that was the first and last time Matthew climbed a tree!

"But He knoweth the way that I take: when He hath tried me, I shall come forth as gold."

Job 23:10

Chapter 6

His Ways Are Higher

For a few years, life was pretty normal. There were no major events, just the ordinary ball games, family gatherings and occasional vacation time. The boys seemed to be healthy and life was good. The years slipped by one by one and my baby boy was now eight years old. Our boys were eight, ten, and twelve: I would soon have a teenager in the house.

I began to be very sick with nausea, and started having some issues with my monthly cycle. I never had any problems and was always very punctual so I was pretty upset and confused about what was going on. I visited my gynecologist, and he could not seem to figure out what was happening.

For two weeks I kept having problems, so I decided to go to my old family doctor. Boy, did I get a surprise! He informed me I was pregnant. I could not believe it. We thought our family was complete. The doctor also told me to go back to my gynecologist and get the IUD removed or I was going to lose my baby. I was in a state of disbelief but did as instructed. I did not need this gynecologist if he was not smart enough to recognize I was pregnant.

I continued seeing Dr. Walter Crawford, who had delivered all three of our boys. He predicted our little bundle of joy's birthday perfectly. Our beautiful daughter, Melissa, was welcomed into our home in August 1977. She weighed a whopping 9lbs 1oz and was the biggest baby of our four. My craving for Snicker candy bars could have contributed to the birth weight. She was incredibly beautiful, though, and she was the only baby in the family for a long time.

We spoiled her and Larry could not believe we had a little girl after three boys. We had given up hope of having a little girl, but God saw things we could not see and blessed us with our baby girl. With what lay in store for our three boys, the gift of a daughter was indeed a miracle! God was so good to bless us with a daughter. We loved our three boys dearly, but we really wanted a little girl.

Larry's sister, Helen, kept Melissa while I worked and over several months, became attached to our new addition. Melissa became the center of Helen's world and filled a place in her life. She helped me tremendously as I was hesitant to leave my baby girl at a day care. I was a little older, thirty as a matter of fact, and was not so keen on day care centers. I felt more comfortable when a close member of the family could keep her.

Our children were very fortunate to have relatively normal childhoods. The boys enjoyed Little League ball and Boy Scouts and acquired lots of friends. Melissa loved Girl Scouts and at the age of eight, she began piano lessons with Suzanne Bowman. Suzanne told her that some piano students have the ability to become a good pianist, but she said Melissa had the ability to become a great pianist. I was incredibly proud her teacher felt she had that kind of ability. After three years of piano, Melissa decided she did not want to take lessons anymore. I felt forcing her would not work, so she quit her lessons.

I was disappointed, but after a few years Melissa decided to take piano again with another teacher. Her new teacher was Demetra Carney from Columbia, Mississippi. Demetra was a very accomplished musician and I was excited Melissa wanted to resume her piano lessons. This would prove to be a blessing because years later a new church was forming and she became the pianist for the new church. Melissa excelled at whatever she chose to do. I am incredibly proud of our sweet and talented daughter. She is not only smart, but beautiful inside and out.

"Trust in the Lord with all thine heart; and lean not unto thine own understanding."

Proverbs 3: 5

Chapter 7

It's Okay, Son

Michael Larry
1983

When our oldest son, Michael, finished high school, he wanted to go to Sullivan Vo-Tech, located in Bogalusa, Louisiana, to continue his education. He graduated high school in 1983 from Tylertown High School in Tylertown, Mississippi. My mom lived in Bogalusa, Louisiana and agreed that Michael could stay with her to attend school. He completed his two year course in electronics, but then decided to go to school at Southwest Community College in Summit, Mississippi. This was the same college his dad attended some years before. Someone convinced him offshore oil was the way to earn some money. After several months at college, the opportunity came for him to go to work with an offshore oil company. In the fall of 1985, he left school and went offshore.

This incident was monumental in Mike's life in many ways. I am so glad as a mother, I did not ridicule or criticize him for the events that happened. He was on the job about three days and one evening, my phone rang. It was Mike. "Mom, come get me!" were the first words I heard.

"Son, what's wrong?" I asked, as usually they stayed at least seven days and he was only about half-way through his time.

"I cannot do this job. Will you please come get me?" I could tell by the tone of his voice he was desperate.

"I'll be right there, son," I answered. "As soon as I can get ready, I will be on my way. Tell me where to come." I hung up the phone and told Larry we had to go get Mike.

"What's wrong?" Larry asked.

"I do not know, he said he could not take it and I am going to get him." I replied. We headed toward Golden Meadow, Louisiana to bring our son home. It was around six in the evening when we left home. We had a very long drive ahead of us. I did all the driving and after several hours, we finally reached the small town of Golden Meadow, Louisiana. The streets were empty and just before I reached the outskirts of this small town, I noticed a blue light flashing behind me. Oh no! I thought. I did not think I was speeding, but I pulled over since there was no one else on the street.

I rolled my window down as the officer approached and his first words were, "Please step out of the car." I opened my door and did as instructed.

"Officer, I did not think I was speeding." I said. Larry was getting out of the car as well.

"You were doing forty in a thirty," the officer countered. At the time, when you got pulled over, you could pay the officer and go ahead. I had no extra money so I knew I could not give him money. This practice has since been stopped due to the police officers taking advantage of people, taking their money, and destroying the ticket. We continued to talk to the officer and told him we were on our way to get our son and finally he put his ticket pad away and let us go.

I was so glad he did not give me a ticket. I was pretty amazed he would even consider giving me a ticket. I was only going 40 mph and there was no traffic around. We continued heading south from Golden Meadow until we reached our destination, and we picked up our very tired and exhausted son. The Muscular Dystrophy was affecting him but we had no knowledge about what he was battling. I am so glad we loved him enough not to question his motives; to trust that he needed to come home. I am glad we did not tell him to tough it out. I am glad we did not tell him he could do it, that he could make it. The truth is, he would not and could not make it. God knew that! I do not think anyone could have been happier than Mike was that night to see his way out of an intolerable situation.

We headed home and again, I was driving. It was around one o'clock in the morning. Again, as I was about to exit the little town of Golden Meadow on the journey home, and again noticed blue lights behind me. This can't be happening! I thought to myself as I pulled over to the side of the road. Same scenario! I got out and the exact same words came out of the officer's mouth.

"You were doing forty in a thirty." The officer said. This was a different officer, though, and not nearly as kind.

"Officer, I'm sorry, I did not realize I was speeding." I tried to reason with him, but he was hearing none of my pleadings. He wanted us to give him money right then. "I do not have extra money." I explained, but nothing seemed to convince the officer. "Larry, come back tomorrow and you can deal with this then." I said to my husband, who was trying to explain also. I was so tired and exhausted that going to jail and lying down was okay with me. If there was no reasoning with this man, then I was ready to get it over with and let my husband and son go home and come back the next day with the money the officer was demanding.

When the officer saw I was serious and he was going to have to take me to jail, he backed off. He finally released us to go on our way. The sun was coming up when we finally arrived home. I can truthfully say, I do not think I have ever been that tired in my life. The mental stress as well as the long drive had really exhausted me. I was glad to have my son safe at home, and my words to him were: "It is okay, son!" Everything happens for a reason. That was not the job God wanted you to have."

Chapter 8

Tragedy Strikes

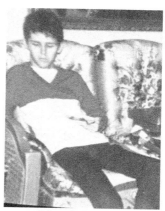

Matthew Lee
1987

Matthew was now sixteen and got into some trouble at school. Larry was not at home much these days since he had invested in some trucks and was on the road much of the time. I felt things were getting beyond my control. I contacted the Lighthouse Ranch for Boys, in Loranger, Louisiana and inquired into the program they offered. The Lighthouse Ranch was a place for troubled young men to get God in their lives while attending school and learning a work ethic. I had heard many good things about the Ranch. I knew the Ranch was affiliated with the church I attended, so I felt they could help Matthew with the problems he was having.

Matthew was not a bad child at all. At his age many young people go through some type of rebellion. He felt some jealousy after Melissa came along. To be honest, we probably did need to give him more attention. It was not intentional, but children have a way of getting your attention if you do not find the time to fulfill their needs. We did not know Matthew felt neglected. After talking to Larry, and to the Ranch, we decided a year at the Ranch was what Matthew needed.

Mom and Dad were not on board, and were very unhappy we made this decision. Within the first week, Matthew ran away from the Ranch. He called and we picked him up at a store he had walked to. After we brought him home and talked with him, he decided to go back and stay for the year. Brother Jim Yohe was the director of the Lighthouse Ranch for Boys. After we took him back, Matthew began to adjust to his new life at the Ranch. We went to see him regularly and he was finding God to be real in his life. The rebellion we had dealt with disappeared. Matthew became very close to many of the staff at the Ranch.

The phone rang one day and it was Brother Yohe. "Sister, I have some bad news." He went on to tell me that Matthew was mowing the grass at the Ranch and had slipped down. His foot went under the mower and he suffered some severe cuts to his foot and toes. Brother Yohe gave me the name of the hospital, so we immediately rushed there to learn the extent of the injuries. Many times when there is no diagnosis of Muscular Dystrophy, accidents happen. With a diagnosis, it simply explains why. Matthew would not have been allowed to do this type of work at the Ranch if his health condition had been known.

When we arrived, the hospital was preparing to transfer him to New Orleans to a bigger hospital. He was going to need extensive surgery on his foot. We followed the ambulance and waited a tense nine hours before they wheeled him into surgery. The doctor came out and talked to us, telling us the first three toes on his right foot were badly injured. His big toe was severed, being held on by a tendon. I was not expecting such a grim diagnosis. I thought he just had to be stitched up. I knew the cuts were bad but to hear the extent of his injuries was depressing. After surgery the doctor informed us they had sewn his toes back on, but there was a real possibility he would still lose them. Only time would tell if Matthew would be able to keep his three toes on his right foot.

Matthew was in the hospital for several days, and finally was able to come home. He was doing amazingly well. On our next visit, the doctor told us it was looking really good and he thought Matthew was going to be able to keep his toes. He also told us he was pretty amazed Matthew did not lose them. He said even though he sewed his big toe back on, he did not expect it to work. Again, God came to our rescue. Thank you, Lord Jesus, for being our God and our friend!

Matthew recuperated at home for a period of time, until he was released from medical care and after two months he returned to the Ranch to finish his year. He was growing into a very Godly and wonderful young man. He was growing closer to God and after second guessing our decision to send him to the Ranch, we determined it was exactly the right decision.

Matthew was feeling a call to the ministry. How awesome! He finished his year and came home a very changed young man. He started going to Powell's Grove United Pentecostal Church where his older brother, Michael, was attending. Michael felt there was a great core of young people who would help keep Matthew rooted and grounded in the Word.

This was in September of 1986, and Matthew soon found a young lady whom he thought God created just for him. This young lady was Kathy Thornhill. Kathy and Matthew had known each other all their lives. When Matthew returned home from the Ranch, they started dating. They would attend church and church events together. They were young, ages sixteen and seventeen, so Kathy's mom and I kept pretty close track of them.

A month after Matthew returned home, Marilyn, Kathy's mom, asked if I wanted to make a quick weekend trip to the Smoky Mountains to see the fall colors. I immediately accepted and we left on Friday. Saturday night around midnight, I received another phone call. This time it was from Larry, telling me Matthew had been in a car wreck. My first question was, "How bad is it?" Larry told me he was being transferred from Tylertown Hospital to Forrest General in Hattiesburg, Mississippi. He said he had a broken leg and he needed more advanced medical care.

I was alarmed, but in my mind I told myself a broken leg could be fixed and he would be fine. We left immediately and drove all night to get to the hospital. I was not prepared for what awaited me when I walked into the room! There were tubes everywhere. My husband had minimized the injuries to me so I would drive safely to get home. Matthew had gone into a coma. He had a closed head injury and his brain was swelling. His lung was punctured, his facial bones were broken, his collar bone was broken and his right leg was a mess! The fat from the bone marrow got into his bloodstream and went to his brain.

The neurosurgeon called Larry and me aside and told us there was absolutely nothing they could do but wait. They could not take him into surgery because he was in a coma. His heart was beating over two hundred beats per minute because the fat emboli had gone to the part of his brain that controlled his breathing and heart rate. The doctor told us if it were a blood clot in the brain, he could operate, but with the fat embolism, he could not. He also told us it could kill him now, or down the road. I was having a hard time wrapping my mind around all this information! I had never heard of a fat embolism.

The doctor told us about a football player in Florida who had suffered a severe break in his ankle and had suffered the same result. The fat from the bone marrow entered into the blood stream. It was fatal for the Florida football player. I began to see just how serious the situation was. The doctors were trying to prepare us for our son's death. They were expecting him to die at any time. We were informed that according to the EEG test on his brain, Matthew had no brain activity. It seemed the situation could not get any worse.

After a week of battling for his life, the doctor told us to go in and we could stay with him as long as we wanted. Larry and I knew they were convinced he was not going to make it. He was still in a coma. We went to his bedside and began to pray. I left the ICU room after a while and made my way to the hospital's small chapel. There was a Bible on a stand in that little room. I removed the Bible, opened it and began to search God's Word for comfort of some kind. I was not ready to let my son go. He was only seventeen!

I placed the open Bible on the floor and knelt on the floor with my face in the pages of that Bible. I began to talk to the One True God. I began to pour out my anguish to the Master! I cried for a time, begging God to touch my son and not to take him. I do not know how long I was in that little chapel, but when I felt calmness in my soul, I returned to the ICU. Larry said, "Ann, I believe he can hear me!" Matthew had been unresponsive and according to his EEG, there was no brain activity. God intervened. Matthew came out of his coma. Praise God for another miracle! Thank, you, wonderful God of Heaven and Earth. God heard my prayer.

There were numerous doctors who were working with Matthew. Since he suddenly awoke from his coma, the surgical team decided they would all work on him at the same time. He had to have some facial surgery and a tremendous amount of work on his right leg. I insisted they leave a prayer cloth on his head that our pastor, Bro. Bobby Spears, brought to us. Matthew was not out of the woods according to the medical staff but there was so much prayer going forth I felt he was going to make it. There were so many preachers coming to pray for him, the ICU staff had to limit the amount of people visiting. Matthew made it through his surgeries. He stayed a few more weeks in the hospital but by the grace of God, he was alive! Matthew was in the hospital for thirty-one days and lost fifty pounds. He was not large before his accident, so he was very frail when he left the hospital. Everyone agreed he was a walking miracle.

After being home for two weeks, Matthew had to go for a check-up and was immediately put him back into the hospital. The doctor told us he had developed osteomyelitis. I had no idea what this was. I had never heard of it. The doctor explained it was an incurable bone disease that would have to be treated with IV antibiotics. Matthew was such a trooper, and did not grumble or complain. He was in the hospital for another month and celebrated his eighteenth birthday while in the hospital. It was definitely not the eighteenth birthday he had imagined, but at least he was alive. He was given as much antibiotics as he could take. He had been through so much. He was so weak and pale.

It was heart wrenching to see him attempting to get around on his leg. Matthew could not bend his right leg more than forty five degrees or about half way. The knee was too damaged. While he was still in the hospital, his IV came out while he was asleep. Matthew woke up and blood was everywhere! It scared him pretty badly, but he summoned the nurse and she scrambled to fix the problem.

Matthew was changed after his wreck. His memory was affected and I could tell he was a different young man. After coming home, we gave him a

55

birthday party. We were thankful to have him with us. Matthew was grateful to be home, but struggled from that time on with medical issues. The genetic monster that was contributing to so many issues with Matthew was still hidden. At the time we did not know about this cruel disease. I am convinced Muscular Dystrophy played a major role in Matthew's accidents. Falling asleep without realizing it is a symptom of Dystrophy but we had no idea at the time.

As Matthew slowly recuperated and regained some normalcy in his life, he began to think about his future. He was eighteen and we knew college was out of the question because of his brain injury. He wanted to go to work, but with his right leg being so damaged and his other limitations, the availability of jobs was very limited. He finally got a job at Popeye's Fried Chicken. The manager was very kind but Matthew had much difficulty trying to do anything that required him to bend his leg. His cognitive skills prevented him from doing the register and his physical limitations hindered him with the manual labor. He soon had to leave this job.

Matthew lied on his application with another company, Asplundh, and got hired. I did not know much about this company or what they did. I would have tried to convince him not to even try to work for Asplundh if I had known. Asplundh was a tree trimming company and the work with them was very difficult even for someone who had no limitations. He tried so hard, but he could not do this job. I am very thankful he did not get injured. Thank you Lord Jesus for our God Moment Miracles.

He was becoming very depressed when there

seemed to be nothing he could do. He applied to Brown and Root Construction Co. and lied on the application to get hired. He worked for a little while, but they soon recognized his limitations and let him go. I watched him lose one job after another, and the deep depression he was sinking into. I sat down with him and we talked. I told him I knew how hard he had tried to work and I admired him so much for trying. I shared how I felt and told him it was time for him to accept that he was disabled. I said if he kept on lying on applications and getting hired on jobs he could not do, he was going to get hurt badly or get killed. I hated to go in this direction but there was no alternative. He reluctantly agreed and I helped him file for disability. It was very hard for a young man only twenty-one years old to accept he was disabled for the rest of his life.

"In everything give thanks: for this is the will of God in Christ Jesus concerning you."

1 Thessalonians 5:18

Chapter 9

Something Is Wrong

Larry Smith

Larry had suffered with polio when he was a child, but he had always been very athletic and kept himself in great shape. His love of basketball did not dissipate when he finished his college career. He continued to play ball when and where he had an opportunity. He played with church and independent teams. Larry would jog a three mile route every day around the lake located close to where we lived. Sometimes I would join him, although my participation was limited to walking. I loved to walk, but running did not interest me. I remember once Larry said, "Why don't you ride a bike so you can keep up with me." I tried that. I rode the bike and the first hill I came to, I had to push the bike up the hill. By the time we made it home, I decided I would continue my slow pace and Larry could run.

When Larry was in his mid-forties, I began to notice some changes. He could not jog as far, and I could tell his stamina was decreasing. I dismissed this by telling myself we were getting to be middle-aged and of course we should start slowing down. My husband was beginning to have problems with going to sleep. He would go to sleep the instant he stopped. He was driving trucks at the time and I told myself he was not getting enough sleep. For each symptom of Myotonic Muscular Dystrophy he displayed, I found a reasonable explanation. I had absolutely no idea how sick my husband was.

When Larry was gone I had to walk alone. A brutal murder had occurred at the lake where we often walked. We always walked down a little cut-off road where a couple of houses were located. Some of our neighbors we knew better than others. One of our neighbors had moved to the country from New Orleans, Louisiana. Our new neighbors had inherited the house and had not lived there very long. They owned a German shepherd which was always kept behind the chain link fence that surrounded the yard. On this particular day, I decided to put the small twenty-five automatic pistol in my skirt pocket since thoughts of the recent murder were still in the fore front of my mind. A young girl was killed and to my knowledge, the murderer was never caught. Law enforcement suspected it was connected to some kind of drug deal.

As I walked past the first house, with the dog, I did not give it a second thought. We never had a problem with the dog being loose. After passing the two houses on this road, I decided not to go the entire route since it was so secluded. I turned around after about a mile and started toward home. As I passed the second house on my way back, I turned around to glance at the gate. To my amazement, the gate was open and the dog was standing there, looking at me. I am terrified of dogs, so he probably smelled my fear, even at several yards away.

The dog immediately started running toward me. I knew he was going to attack! I barely had time to reach into my skirt pocket to pull out the small hand gun. I quickly turned the safety off and aimed the gun. The dog was within ten yards of me. Pointing toward the ground in front of the dog, I fired a shot! I did not aim to hit the dog; I simply wanted to scare him. That is exactly what happened. The dog came to a screeching halt, then turned and ran back into the yard. I was glad I did not have to fire the second shot which would have been aimed directly at the dog.

When I got home, I was pretty shaken by these unwelcome events. That was the first time I had carried a gun with me on my walks. I could count on one hand the times I had even fired a gun. Thinking of what could have happened that morning made me shudder. This was another God Moment in my life. That was the first and last time I have ever carried a gun while walking.

I called the dog's owner and explained to him what happened. He was very upset that I had fired a shot toward his dog. I was angered that he was threatening to file charges on me for firing a shot at his dog. He was not at all concerned for my safety. I told him to do what he had to do, but he could be assured if his dog was not confined, the next shot would not be pointed toward the ground! Needless to say, we were not close friends, especially after this incident.

One night my phone rang and it was a call from Larry. He said, "I wanted to let you know I had a really close call tonight."

"What do you mean?" I asked. He continued to tell me he had crashed through a bridge rail, plunging into a lake. "How did that happen? Are you alright?" I asked. He explained that he was shaken, but almost did not make it out of the truck before it sank. Larry was always a great swimmer and this time it saved his life. He managed to get the window down and crawled through it with no time to spare. It was in the middle of the night and thankfully the place he landed was near enough he swam to shore.

There were so many questions about how and why this happened. I did not put the puzzle pieces together until many years later. I feel he simply went to sleep for a few moments. God had His hand on my husband that night. In each near tragedy, I can see angels encamped around my family. This could have ended very differently. If Larry had not been the athletic person he was, and with the Muscular Dystrophy beginning to become evident, he could have lost his life. Again, God, you are such a friend, comforter and are always mindful of your children.

In the summer of 1987 I was working at an exercise salon in McComb, Mississippi. A friend of mine, Marilyn, had opened a salon and asked me to run it. I was keeping fit and having fun while helping others to be healthier. I enjoyed my job.

Before leaving for home one night, I received a phone call. I do not remember who called, but I was informed that Larry and Melissa had been involved in an accident. They were in McComb and were going home after we had eaten dinner. I could not get a lot of details, but the wreck happened just outside of Tylertown, Mississippi and they were taken to the local hospital. A few minutes later, I received another call, telling me to go to the hospital in McComb, Mississippi because they were transferring Melissa.

The information I received was that Melissa had a pretty bad cut on her leg and Larry had several facial cuts and a bruised chest. I rushed to the hospital where Melissa was brought in soon after I arrived. She was conscious but was in a mild state of shock. She did not remember anything about the wreck. She knew she was hurt, but not how badly. The doctor came into the room and when they revealed her leg, I gasped. I did not want to alarm Melissa, but her leg was a mess. She was rushed into surgery and the doctor came out to tell us he had to do inner and outer stitches. He also said if her cut had been any deeper, it would have cut into the artery. All I could think was, "Thank you, God, one more time!"

Melissa still has some ugly scars on her leg. Skin grafting and a lot of repair work was needed to minimize the scars, but that was minor compared to her life. She was nine years old and later told me how embarrassed she was at how her leg looked. Wearing a bathing suit because of her ugly scars was hard for her. At the time, I was rebounding from Matthew's horrific wreck and I was so thankful their lives had been spared; I could not see the emotional impact this accident had on my baby girl.

Larry was treated and released from the hospital but I felt he should have been kept in the hospital. He seemed to be hurt more than he realized and more than the ER staff acknowledged. I picked glass from his face for days after he got home. With all the information gathered about the wreck, it led me to believe Larry went to sleep behind the wheel again. He left the road and hit a car coming out of a side road. There were no injuries in the other vehicle, thankfully. It was becoming clear to me that my husband did not need to be behind the wheel of a vehicle. Convincing him would be another matter. No one in their forties wants to admit they need to quit driving, especially when driving is the way they make their living.

After Larry recuperated, I convinced him he needed to get out of the trucking business. He changed jobs, but his next line of work had him on the road just as much, in a car instead of a big truck. Since we had no idea about the Muscular Dystrophy, he continued trying to work. He went into the insurance business, and was quite good at being a salesman. This was surprising to me. I never pictured him as a salesman.

Larry managed to continue with a daily routine but I could see something was wrong. I could not figure out what was happening to him. It was getting harder and harder for him to get up in the morning to get his day started. I think he was beginning to wonder what was going on, but he was doing the same thing I was: try to find ways to excuse or to rationalize what was happening.

"I will lift up mine eyes unto the hills, from whence cometh my help."

Psalms 121:1

Chapter 10

Angels all Around Us

On January 1, 1990, it was a cold and rainy day. I had the privilege of coming into contact with some total strangers whom I will always believe God put into my path. I traditionally cook a huge meal on New Year's Day and this was no exception. I invited my friend, Marilyn and her daughter, Kathy, to come eat our holiday meal with us. The meal was almost ready, but at the last minute, I realized I needed something from the store. We lived about five miles from town and Marilyn said, "I will go with you. Let's go in my van."

We headed to the grocery store. Before we got there, I noticed some people walking in the cold, rainy weather. There were two adults and two small children. We passed them and went to the store, but I could not get these people out of my mind. I kept seeing the picture of those small children in the rain. I told Marilyn I wanted to try to find them to see if we could help them. At first, she thought this was not a good idea. Her comment was, "We do not know these people. I think we should go home."

Something was compelling me to find these people and help them. I did not realize it, but later, after reflecting on this event, I felt it was a God Moment. My feeling was so compelling that I told my friend, "If you do not want to stop, take me home and I will get my car and come back." She reluctantly agreed to stop and we found the cold, wet strangers and pulled over. I know this can be dangerous, but I assure you, I felt I must help these tired, weary strangers.

When we stopped, I asked them if we could help them in some way. They said their car had broken down and they had been on the road for some time. I did not get their whole story at the time. I told them to get in the van and they could come to my house for a hot meal. That was my intention; to get them dried off and give them a hot meal. They were so cold and I found out the woman was pregnant. Their car was left two states away. They were broke, wet, cold and trying to get home to Texas. That was a long way from where we were in Louisiana.

We found dry clothes for them and fed them a hot meal. I felt I had not missed it in picking them up. They had a little girl who was close to my daughter in age. Melissa shared some of her Christmas toys with the little girl. My heart went out to these people who were destitute. There was a possibility of some snow for the night so my next thought was, "What now?" I could not see turning these people out on the street in the cold. I asked my friend Marilyn, "How can we help these people?" Marilyn had decided to help, so we got busy figuring out how to do that.

We decided to get in touch with the Salvation Army in McComb, Mississippi to see if they could provide shelter for the night. The next order of business was to get enough money to buy them a bus ticket home. That is exactly what we did. Marilyn lived in Summit, Mississippi, which is close to McComb, so dropping them off at the Salvation Army was on her way home. I gathered all the information I could get from this family so I could keep track of them and make sure they arrived home. I contacted the Pentecostal church in Jackson, Mississippi to see if they would go to the bus station and check on them.

I never heard from them again. There was no trace of them. I have the assurance in my heart I did exactly what God wanted me to. So many people told me I was scammed. Maybe I was. In case this was a test from the Master, I feel I passed. The compassion I showed to this family did not cost me much, so I am better for it, regardless of what their intentions were. They did not ask me to stop. God did!

Some people do not believe in angels, but I know they are all around us. Recently, my wonderful grandson, Mark Scott, related an event that occurred in his own personal life. For years he had been struggling with insecurities about his worthiness to enter Heaven and dwell with God. Satan attacked him over and over. He would seem to get victory, but in the course of time, those haunting thoughts would return to him. I and many others fasted and prayed for healing and for Mark Scott to have the peace of mind we knew God wanted for him.

While visiting my daughter and staying with my grandchildren for Melissa and Baron to have a weekend getaway, I was sitting at the kitchen table one morning and heard someone enter. I turned to see my grandson coming toward me. "Nana, I saw an angel last night." he stated with a somewhat calm voice.

"Really?" I asked. "Tell me about it." I said to him as he seated himself next to me at the table.

"I woke up last night and there was an angel at the foot of my bed toward my closet. There was a man standing close to my door. I do not know who the man was." I listened as he continued. "It was kind of weird. The angel would move a little toward the man then disappear! The angel would reappear a little closer to the man each time. I watched this and at first I was afraid, but then I felt a deep peace as I watched the angel reach the man. Those huge wings that seemed to fill the room, wrapped around the man."

I was feeling the awesome presence of God. I knew this was not a vivid imagination. I knew my grandson had experienced a heavenly visit! I asked Mark what the angel looked like. He began to describe the brightness of the angel and I felt excitement that God had allowed Mark to find such favor with him. I wanted to know what Mark felt all this meant. I asked him, "Mark, what do you feel this means?

"Nana, I don't know. I know I felt very peaceful as I watched the angel." Knowing how long and hard he had battled the fear that kept invading his mind, I could not help but believe God had sent him an angel to give him a measure of comfort and peace. I told him that. I told him if he ever experienced fear again, to bring this experience back to mind and feel the peace and calmness God brought to him during this incredible visitation from an angel. I also told him he had to be highly favored of God to be given this personal confirmation!

"Be not forgetful to entertain strangers: for thereby some have entertained angels unawares."

Hebrews 13:2

Chapter 11

Changing Direction

Deidra, Mary, Janie, Ann

After Larry had worked for a couple of years in insurance, he said, "Ann, you would be good in insurance." I had held a variety of jobs over the years including bookkeeping, retail sales, and management, but after giving it some thought, I decided he was right. I wanted to try it. I accepted a position with Security Plan Insurance located in Bogalusa, Louisiana. I made most of the conventions and was able to travel to Toronto, Canada and several trips to Las Vegas. I won numerous awards during the twelve years with this company, including agent of the year in our district office more than once. This was a job I enjoyed and excelled in. I was also able to travel to Hawaii and Cancun, Mexico while working with a different company as an independent agent.

This was a period of joy and contentment in our lives, despite the earlier tragedies. Within a couple of years, I was promoted to sales manager. The District manager and I had some differences and I was transferred to another district. I had to travel to Slidell to work and had a broad territory with five agents to manage. I did it for several years, but when they split the Bogalusa District and I had a chance to go back to Bogalusa, I was elated. My manager in Slidell was transferred to Bogalusa, so that was great. I had to give it up in 2002 because of family and health issues.

In 1992, we decided to sell our home in Tylertown, Mississippi and move to Bogalusa, Louisiana so we could be close to our work. We started looking for a house to buy. We owned a black Jaguar which mistakenly gave the impression we had plenty of money. We had purchased this fine car from a preacher friend of ours and there was a certain amount of looks you got as you rode down the street. We were far from

74

rich, however, and when the real estate agent took us to view a beautiful two story house situated on the banks of the Pearl River cut off, I thought it was out of our price range. I fell in love with this big two story home. We lived in a 1400 square foot home for twenty years, so this 3500 square foot home was like touring a mansion. There were two and a half acres of beautiful yard. It had an intercom system, a laundry chute from upstairs to the laundry room downstairs and a beautiful office with built in cabinets. There was not a down side to this property.

As I was driving out of the driveway of this gorgeous home, I was mentally thinking, I should tell Molly, the real estate agent, we cannot afford this home. I was going over in my mind what I was going to say to convince her to show us some lower priced homes when God spoke to me. This scripture came to me so forcefully I had to acknowledge it to be God. "YOU HAVE NOT BECAUSE YOU ASK NOT." I began to question God: "Okay, God, is this really possible?" The more I thought about it, the more I talked to the Lord. I certainly did not want to buy something I would lose down the road.

The agent called me the next day and said, "Well, what did you think?"

I replied, "Molly, the house is absolutely gorgeous, but I think it's a little more than we can afford." You would have to know Molly to understand why she is such a dynamic sales person. She was totally undaunted!

She said, "You know, I feel this is the house for you. Let's get together and see exactly what you can do and we will go from there." That is what we did. Molly asked what we could do on a down payment on the house. After talking with the owner, the terms were agreed upon and we purchased our dream home in August 1992. My daughter thought this was her birthday present since her birthday was on the eighteenth of August. I know material things do not bring true happiness, but I also know God has no problem with His people having nice things. It was the Master that made it all possible. Thank you, Jesus, for watching out for our needs, and in this case our wants.

I was unaware at the time of how much God was present in the purchase of our beautiful home. Larry's disease was progressing rapidly, and we still had no idea he was dealing with a debilitating disease. We did not have a diagnosis, but by this time it was evident to me something was going on. Larry was beginning to have obvious difficulty walking and it seemed he was getting slower and slower. His speech was affected. We still did not seek any specialized care or treatment. The changes were slow, and Larry shrugged them off when I would mention anything to him. For several more years we did what we always did. Larry was doing his best to go to work every day. I know it must have been extremely hard to do at times. He had given up on any type of exercise because he gained weight and could not do it.

By this time in our lives, our three boys were grown and gone. Michael had married the love of his life, Shelia Lee, and they welcomed two wonderful children into our family. Whitney Leigh and Michael Ray were the sunshine in my oldest son's life. He absolutely adored his children. Marcus, our middle son had also married and given us a grandson, Erik. Erik was our first grandchild. He was born on September 30, 1983. Seven years later along came Whitney on February 6, 1990. Michael Ray was born on July 27, 1992. March 27, 1995 Melissa had her first child, Mark Scott. Life was moving right along. Matthew had medical problems that we dealt with as each situation would arise. Marcus was so small, but he seemed to be doing okay.

Melissa graduated from Bogalusa High School in May, 1995. She had married but still wanted to continue her education. She attended Pearl River Community College until her short marriage came to an abrupt end. Suffice it to say through no fault of hers, she had to end the marriage. We know God wants us to be partners for life, but sometimes that is not possible. She married too young and the marriage had a slim chance of survival. She thought everything would be beautiful but it did not work out that way.

God had another plan for her life and I am so glad He sent the most wonderful man into her life. They both live for God and work diligently in their church. Baron is a computer programmer and also holds seminars for Crown Financial. Melissa and Baron have two wonderful children together, Alissa Gabriella and Seth Gabriel. Mark Scott was adopted by his step-dad, Baron. I love my family so very much. God has shown me how precious family and life are.

Melissa related a God Moment in her life. She was driving behind a truck filled with wooden pallets. The truck was stacked as high as it could be. Several times she tried to go around the truck but the two lane road she was traveling was noted for accidents so there was no way to go around the truck. Finally she felt she could move into the other lane and go around. As she moved into the other lane, the pallets came loose and barely missed hitting her windshield. They were all over the road behind her as she looked into her rear view mirror. She could only contemplate what would have happened if she had been only a few seconds later moving into the other lane. Was this a coincidence? We feel it was not. We choose to recognize every God Moment in our life.

I challenge you to take a look at your own life. Think about the times you felt you were incredibly lucky. Was it luck or was it a God Moment?

Chapter 12

God Has Talked To Me

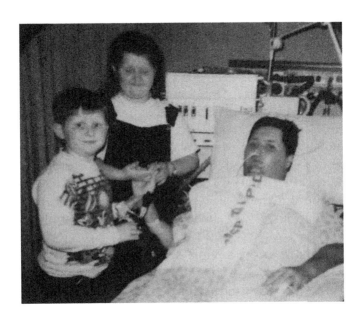

Michael Ray, Whitney and Michael

My oldest son, Michael, had been having some problems in the months leading up to the date of November 15, 1998, He was struggling with a truck driving job. His father-in-law owned the truck he was driving. He had several small mishaps, nothing major, but all the little things were beginning to make Ray question whether he had done the right thing in hiring Mike to drive a truck. He had backed into a ditch, and had several little events that could have been major.

One day when Mike was loading his truck close to our house, he called. Since he had to wait a while to get loaded, he decided to come for a short visit. We were always happy with any time we could spend with him. When he came, we always tried to pamper him a little, and he looked forward to coming to Mama's house to enjoy a meal with us.

Mike was pretty large and he did love to eat. Most of the people in our family have the same favorite pastime; cooking good food and enjoying it. On this particular day, we were playing a game and invited Mike to join us. If my memory serves me correctly, the game was Pictionary. I noticed Mike as he was trying to guess the drawings. He could not see! I said, "Mike, how long have you been having trouble with your eyes?"

"I have been having some problems for a little while." He replied. I wanted to know how bad his eyes were. I was very alarmed that he was on the road with an eighteen wheeler if he could not see. After questioning him a little further and doing my own testing, I became extremely alarmed.

"Baby, you have to get to a doctor as soon as you get home." In fact, I was worried about him getting home.

"Mom, I do not have any insurance, I cannot afford to go to the doctor." he said.

"Mike, there are organizations that will pay for you some glasses and even for your doctor visit." I countered.

He kind of mumbled, "Okay" and I could see he was getting upset, so I dropped the subject. After we took him back to the mill to get his truck, I immediately called Shelia, his wife.

"Shelia, did you realize Mike cannot see?" I believe those were my exact words. "Please do not let him get back in that truck until he gets his eyes checked." She said she would see to it that he went to the doctor, so I felt a little better. Now, if he can get home safely!

True to her word, Shelia made an appointment and Mike went to see Dr. Henry Sanders in McComb, Mississippi. When they returned home, Shelia called me, "I am glad we got him to the doctor!" she said

After the doctor had examined Mike's eyes. Dr. Sanders said, "I hope he has not been driving." He had no idea this was what he did for a living. "He is legally blind." were his next words. I was completely dumbfounded when I heard Shelia tell me this incredible news.

"You mean he is BLIND?" was my stunned response. I knew he could not see well, but totally blind? No wonder he had been having little mishaps on the truck. He had cataracts on both eyes. He did not get around very quickly, but I thought it was because he was big. In fact, if I could have known and connected the dots, he was behaving just like his Dad. He was having some slurring of speech, weakness in his hands and ankles and cataracts in his thirties. These were all symptoms of a disease they did not know they had at this point.

Shelia confided to me about how she could not understand what was going on with Mike. I could not give her any answers, because I was dealing with the exact same things with Larry. I tried to console her and tell her to hang in there and they had two lovely children. I tried to reassure her somehow God would bring them through.

Mike was so excited to be able to see again after his surgery. He went back to work, but his struggles were becoming evident. Mike was very close to me and had always confided his innermost feelings. We had always been able to talk. He felt a call to the ministry, but due to circumstance, he only preached one short message. I have a tape of this message and it is one of my most prized possessions.

His pastor was Brother Doyle Spears, who at the time was the pastor at Powell's Grove Pentecostal Church in Jayess, Mississippi. Brother Spears was a mentor to Mike as was Brother Earl Carney from Stateline UPC, in Tylertown, Mississippi. These were two very spiritual men who helped shape and mold the character of my son.

Due to all that was happening in Mike's life, he had become very discouraged. He came to our house with his two children to spend the weekend while Shelia went on a business trip. I could tell something was bothering him that weekend and he finally opened up. "Mom, I just do not understand." he said. "It seems the harder I try, the worse things get." He went on, "I have always been faithful to God. I cannot seem to get ahead financially. I don't know what else to do!" My heart as a mother was aching for him. I could feel his pain, but I knew this was a spiritual battle and all I could do was let him know I would help him pray and seek God.

We had an awesome service that weekend at church and during the altar call on Sunday night, November 15, I felt Mike needed to take a trip to the altar and lay his burdens there. I felt this so intensely I went to Mike and asked if he wanted to go pray. His head was bowed, but he shook his head no, and I did not pursue the strong feeling that he needed to pray. If I could have looked into the future just a few hours, I would have never let him leave that place without crying out for God's mercy. If he could have looked into the future just a few hours, I would not have had to ask him. The service ended and we went home.

"Mike, why don't you and the kids stay and get up early in the morning and go home?" I asked. I did not want him to leave.

"I need to get on back tonight," was his reply.

I remember saying, "Baby, be careful, the roads are wet." after he insisted on going home. It was about an hour and a half drive from Bogalusa, Louisiana to outside of Brookhaven, Mississippi where they lived. As I went to bed that night, my heart was so heavy. It was around eleven when I heard the phone ring. Larry was still up so I knew he would answer it, but I sprang out of bed anyway. I knew something was wrong. I walked into the room as Larry was on the phone, "How bad is he?" I heard him say. I just stood there with my eyes fixed on my husband as I was listening to his side of the conversation. "What about the children?"

I could hear the anguish in his voice while he was trying to get as much information as he could. When he hung up the phone, he said, "We have to get to the hospital as soon as we can. Mike and the children have been in a wreck. The children are banged up pretty badly, but they had to cut Mike out with the jaws-of-life. They are in Monticello right now, but are preparing to transfer him to Jackson to University Hospital."

I knew it was bad. I began to pray in my mind as I hurriedly got dressed, "God, please be with him! Please don't take him! Not now!" I know so many loved ones have cried out this prayer to God.

We entered the hospital in Monticello, Mississippi just as they were wheeling Mike out of the ER into a waiting ambulance. I do not think he even knew we were there although his eyes were open. "Baby, we are here, everything will be alright. You hang in there." I kept repeating. The ambulance crew did not even slow the stretcher down as they rushed past us. "We'll be behind you." I commented as they closed the doors and left. Again, all I could do was pray, "God, please be with my Mike and put your hand on him." I had to drive because Larry was past being able to. I knew I could not keep up with the ambulance, so I drove as fast as I could.

The ER staff was already working on Mike when we got there and we were there but a very short time when a doctor came out and talked with us. "He has internal bleeding, and from the x-rays, it looks like we may be dealing with a torn aorta. His blood pressure is very low. He is having trouble breathing, and we are heading to surgery. We will keep you informed." With those words, the doctor left and we were left to try to grasp some kind of hope. I was numb! "This cannot be happening!" I wanted to scream, "God, where are you? Please, dear God, please do not let him die!"

I was just whispering incoherent words to God. I could not comfort Larry and he could not comfort me. We had been through so much with Matthew and now it looked as though we were going to lose Mike. I knew any kind of arterial bleed was very serious because his heart was his lifeline. We would pace and pray, and then sit and pray. Shelia's mom and dad had taken Whitney and Mick to their house when they were discharged from the emergency room, so I knew they were okay. Shelia was scheduled to fly in on Monday. Her sisters decided not to tell her about Mike until after she arrived in McComb so they could be with her.

Time seemed to stand still. I kept looking at the clock and all I could do was keep saying, over and over, "God, please be with him! God, please be with him!" It was about an hour and a half before the doctor came out and said, "I have some good news and bad news. Thankfully, his aorta was not torn as it looked like on the x-ray, but he has severe bruising to his chest and is having a lot of difficulty breathing. We are probably going to have to do a tracheotomy for him to be able to breathe. His spleen was ruptured, and he is definitely not out of the woods!" We could not see him at all that night, but as the doctor left, I knew God had heard our feeble cries for help. I will always believe that Mike's number came up that night and God had mercy. Thank you so much, God, for mercy!

The next day they let us go back to see him. He had this oxygen mask over his face and he was struggling so hard to breathe. His blood pressure kept dropping to a very low rate, and he was still in a critical condition. He was still in the ER. The doctors were waiting to see if his condition would improve to possibly avoid the tracheotomy. Shelia got there and as soon as she did, the doctors told her Mike would have to have the tracheotomy. They were hoping it would be temporary but at this point they could not give a long term prognosis. Mike's diaphragm would not expand enough to allow him to breathe.

He was conscious, but could not talk. His eyes were speaking volumes to me, though. I knew he was desperately fighting for his life! I held his hand and would not allow myself any tears. I knew I had to be strong for him. "Baby, hang in there. Everything's going to be okay." I kept telling him. I certainly did not feel this way, but I had to try to convince him. He was soon taken to surgery and from there to ICU on a ventilator. He was only thirty-three so everyone thought, "He's young, and he will be okay. Just give him a little time. He'll bounce back!"

I will never forget a visit I had with Mike as soon as he was conscious enough to be able to think. He could not talk, but he had improved to the point he could scribble a little on a piece of paper to communicate with us. I knew he wanted to tell me something, and there was a pen and paper by his bed. He motioned for me to get it. He struggled to scribble a note to me, and these were the first words he wrote, "I have been so foolish." I squeezed his hand and said, "Mike, we have all been foolish at one time or another. Do not be hard on yourself. God is your friend and He is going to watch over you." I watched as the tears welled up in his eyes and I knew exactly what he was talking about. I knew that he knew, you cannot question God.

Sometimes it is hard to go through some things life throws at you, but you have to trust God knows what He is doing. That is a very hard lesson for the flesh to learn. I would have traded places with him in a heartbeat. I would have given anything to let him get up out of that bed and go home to his two precious children.

The next visit I made to see Mike, I had barely made it into the room before he motioned for me to get the pen and writing pad. I handed it to him and watched as he scribbled something on the page. It took a lot of figuring things out, but he had a happy look in his eyes this time. As I read his note, I could not hold back the floodgate of emotion that I felt. He had written, "God has talked to me." I knew by his countenance God really had talked to him. Mike received the sweet Holy Ghost when he was twelve years old and was an exemplary child. He never gave me any trouble. He lived for God and never sowed wild oats. He never drank alcohol, did drugs or did many things that young people so often experience. He always made me proud and we had such a sweet bond. I will always treasure the beautiful relationship I had with Mike.

Mike gained some strength, but his hospital stay was beginning to puzzle the doctors. Days turned into weeks and whenever they would try to wean him off the ventilator, he could not breathe. After five long weeks in the hospital ICU, the doctors began to call in more specialists to try to figure out why this young man could not breathe. He should have recuperated enough to be able to breathe on his own. The doctors finally found their answer. They discovered Mike had a hereditary disease known as Myotonic Muscular Dystrophy.

This was extremely shocking news, because there is no cure and the condition only worsens; it never improves. We were all reeling from this diagnosis. When the doctors advised us to get everyone in the family tested, the pieces of a puzzle began to go into place. I knew immediately Larry had it when I learned the symptoms. What I did not know was my other two sons also had this debilitating disease! I think the whole family was in total disbelief and shock. Mike went into a deep depression and I think he was on the verge of giving up. He became very ill. His body became septic and the doctors were not expecting him to live through the night.

I called my brother, Carl, who was in revival at his church at the time. I relayed the dire news and asked him to please pray. Carl asked his son, Nathan, to stand in for Mike for anointing and prayer. The doctor came in the next morning and said, "All I can say is, he must have nine lives." Mike was much better. Again, the God of Heaven heard our cries. Another God Moment Miracle!

I really appreciate my brother, Carl, and his wife Jean, who helped us so much during this very trying time in our lives. They were so sacrificial in their giving and their prayers. There were so many people who were holding us up in prayer. I will be forever grateful to all of you who gave a dollar, bought a CD, and especially to all who bowed your knees and prayed. So many of you sought a miracle for Mike and I know God heard every prayer, but for a reason known only to God, it was not his will to heal Mike.

Mike ministered to so many during his sickness. His sweet spirit and testimony spoke to so many people. He may not have been able to stand in a pulpit and verbally preach another message, but through his sickness, he ministered to all of us. He never again questioned God. He accepted his fate with a grace that amazed me.

After about eight weeks in the ICU, Mike began to have gall bladder attacks. He needed surgery for his gall bladder, but he could not be put to sleep. The doctors were debating how to handle this situation. They finally decided they would have to do a spinal block. There was no other way, although this had a high risk. Doing a spinal block in the lower back is done all the time, but to do it higher in the spinal column puts other vital organs at risk. They were able to do it, and Mike made it over one more hurdle.

We spent Thanksgiving and Christmas in the hospital with Mike. Days turned into weeks, and weeks lapsed into months. I was trying to hold my job, but three days a week, I headed to Jackson, Mississippi to be with my baby. He was thirty-three, but he was still my baby. I would go in and rub his feet. That was the only little bit of comfort I could bring to him, and he grew to expect it when I walked in the door.

When Mike was finally allowed to go home, in February of 1999, he was called a miracle patient by his medical team at University Hospital in Jackson, Mississippi. He was indeed a miracle! This was the best birthday gift he could have given his precious daughter, Whitney, who celebrated her 9th birthday around this time. He had to go home on a ventilator, but he was alive. He never grumbled or complained during his sickness. When God talked to him right after his accident, he never questioned God again. He lived over nine years as a ventilator patient and over five on hospice care, but he never questioned God. He loved his God, gave thanks to his God and had more grace than most of us will ever know.

As Mike left the hospital, the halls were lined with doctors, nurses, and even some patients, to bid him farewell. We were so excited that he was finally able to go home. His tracheotomy had to become permanent and there were still many hurdles to overcome, but we would take it one step at a time. The first hurdle was that he needed two ventilators at home. There would not be time to get another if the first one went out for any reason.

Mike had no insurance. We could not let our minds go in that direction. All of our energy had to be focused on Mike, and we would deal with the bills later. We knew he would never work again, so the hospital had already applied for Medicaid for him. The company that supplied his ventilators did so with no insurance in place and no money. That was a God Moment Miracle!

Mike was set up at home in almost the same setting as he was in the hospital, except he did not have the medical staff to watch him twenty-four-seven. Shelia was a real trooper. She learned everything she could about his disease and was amazing in her care for Mike. We all rallied to them and did what we could. So many people reached out to Mike and Shelia during this time. They had a strong church family that prayed for them constantly.

There were so many adjustments in their household. They went from two incomes to none. Shelia had to quit her job to take care of Mike. It was a full time job to do this since he still required a lot of care. I even learned how to take care of his needs. It was kind of frightening to learn how to put a tube down his windpipe and suction him. I had no medical training, but when you have to do it, you learn. Whitney and Mick were so glad to have their Dad home, but they had been through a lot in the past few months as well. Another God Moment Miracle came when Shelia was able to get a job working from home. I do not know how they would have managed without this blessing.

I thought I knew what trusting God was. I always thought I fully trusted God. I lived the first year Mike was home in a constant state of panic. Every phone call would make me jump; I knew it was going to be the call that told me he was gone. Larry had much more faith than I did. He kept telling me, "Ann, Mike is not going to die." He was right. He did not have to see our son die. I did not know it, but God was going to call Larry home first. Mike managed to live for over nine years after his accident.

We had many alarming situations and some very close calls, but God brought him through each time. I remember one such incident. I got a call from Shelia and she told me she was on her way back to the hospital. Mike could not breathe! She told me not to come right now, that she would call me with news later, after she had more information. What she encountered when she got to the emergency room was nothing short of a nightmare. University Hospital is a teaching hospital and a large part of their staff is students or interns. She tried to explain the gravity of Mike's situation, but the young intern did not seem to get it. He wanted to send Mike back home because they had no room in the ICU. Because of his ventilator status, he could not go into a regular room. Shelia refused to leave and finally they had to admit him!

Shelia tried all night to convince the young intern of how critical Mike was, but to no avail. By six o'clock the next morning when the shift changed and a more experienced doctor came on duty, it was almost too late for Mike. His condition had worsened to the point the doctor had to give him a shot to literally stop his heart. His heart beat was so erratic they could not get it to an even pace. The doctor also told us it was a possibility his heart would not restart. Mike knew that agreeing to do this was life or death. He told me later, "Now I know what it feels like to die!" Needless to say, they made a place for him in ICU.

Shelia reported the intern to the hospital administrator so that hopefully he would be more diligent in his care of sick people. I hope I never have to be treated or cared for by that doctor.

Another close call was when Mike aspirated on some food, causing pneumonia to manifest. Complications with the lungs or the heart is usually what kills a Myotonic Muscular Dystrophy patient. The throat muscles get weak and the patient sometimes cannot swallow their food, causing it to go into the lungs. Many MMD patients have to get a feeding tube because of this danger. Thank God, Mike did not have to get a feeding tube. That was a huge blessing for him to be able to eat and enjoy his food. He had some limitations in his diet, but almost to the end, he could eat.

There was so much Mike needed, but as each need would arise, God would provide. He needed a lift chair, because he was too weak to get up by himself. I remember looking in the buy, sell and trade paper we would pick up each week. We did not have much money left. I was only working part time, Larry was not working much, and as needs arose we would help Mike and Shelia.

I saw an ad in the paper for a lift chair. I called the lady and she wanted three hundred dollars for the chair. It was an oversize chair and it was what Mike needed. I told the lady why I wanted the chair and a little about Mike and what he had been through. The lady said, "Honey, you come and get this chair, you can have it." Wow! I was hoping she would come down on the price, but I did not expect her to give it to us. This was another God Moment! Mike was so excited when we brought his new chair. It was in excellent condition and he got much use from this blessing.

God came through again in the way of a material blessing when Mike and Shelia's stove went out. There was no money to purchase a new one. I called my daughter Melissa, and said, "Do you think you and Baron could pay half for a stove for Mike and Shelia?" They agreed, so I went into a store to price one. I asked the clerk for the best deal he could give me because I was trying to find a stove for my son who was ill.

A lady was standing close by and evidently heard

what I said, because as I was walking to the front of the store, she stopped me. "I overheard you saying you needed a stove for someone in your family who is sick. I have a good electric stove I no longer need. If you will come get it, you can have it." I could have fallen to the floor I was so surprised and extremely thankful.

"You have no idea how much you have blessed my son!" I exclaimed. "Thank you so much and I pray God blesses you tenfold for your generosity." We picked the stove up and it was a far better stove than we were going to buy. Isn't it amazing how much our God is aware of our circumstance? God really taught me how to trust him while going through Mike's sickness.

Mike probably holds the record for the longest length of time being on hospice care. He was on hospice care for over five years. Thank God for the beautiful people who provided such loving care and did so many amazing things to make Mike's life as bright as they could make it. I will never forget Nona Sutton, one of Mike's nurses, and Shannon Hartzog, the social worker with Community Hospice Care in McComb, Mississippi. Shannon had gone to school with Mike, so she was a friend as well.

I do not know whose idea it was, but one day Mike was asked what would be one thing he would like to do if he could do anything he wanted. He loved football, and especially watching the Saints and the Manning boys, Peyton and Eli, play football. His reply was, "I wish I could go see a football game with Peyton or Eli playing." Larry and Mike would talk back and forth on the phone, "Who Dat? Who Dat? Who Dat say they gonna beat dem Saints?" This exchange would go on back and forth when a game was being played. I think Peyton was playing for the Colts at the time Mike was going through his sickness. Mike followed the Saints, but he also followed the Colts and the Giants, who Eli played for.

Nothing was mentioned for a while after Mike was asked the question about what would be something he would like to do, so nothing more was thought about it. Then one day, the hospice team arrived with a football signed by Archie Manning. The football was housed in a nice clear display case. Peyton and Eli had sent 11x14 signed and framed photographs. He was so excited and thrilled they would do this for him. There was a party with cake and all the trimmings!

This beautiful and exciting day soon turned to one filled with anxiety. Mike went to the bathroom and he collapsed to the floor while there. He was large, so there was not much room to try to get him off the floor. The hospice team rushed in to help get Mike up. It took probably thirty minutes to get Mike out of the bathroom. They had to put a blanket on the floor, get him to roll over onto it and pulled him into the hallway before he could be helped to stand. Thank God the hospice team was there. This was surely a God Moment!

Mike was getting so weak, but his desire and will to live was astounding. He was trying so hard to stay here as long as he could. I know this was for his kids. He asked God soon after coming home from the hospital if He could to let him live to see his kids grow up. God allowed that!

I was amazed so many times at how he held on and pulled through when it looked as though it would not happen. A couple of months before Mike went to his eternal home, I was visiting one day and said to him, "Son, do you remember the prayer you prayed when you came home, about letting you see your kids grow up?

He looked at me and kind of smiled, "Yes, I do," he replied.

I said, "You know God has answered that prayer. Whitney will soon be eighteen and Michael will soon be sixteen."

He said with a grin, "I know, but now I think I am going to ask God to let me see my grandkids grow up!" We both knew that would not happen but he never lost his sense of humor. Even when he knew his time was rapidly approaching, he had no fear of death. He knew he would have a new body and he was beginning to want that.

> "And He saith unto them: why are ye fearful, o ye of little faith? Then He arose, and rebuked the winds and the sea; and there was a great calm."
>
> *Matthew 8:26*

Chapter 13

The Nightmare, Katrina

Bogalusa, Louisiana.   August 2005

During hurricane season, in south Louisiana and all along the coastline from Florida to Texas we all keep our eyes and ears open to any news of an approaching storm. We always have some storms; sometimes, we are lucky and do not get any severe ones, but occasionally, we get a monster! This was the case on August 29, 2005. We watched the news for days ahead of time to see where Katrina was going to make landfall.

As the storm approached land, the city of New Orleans began to brace itself for a direct hit. There had not been a direct hit to the city for many years and there was much skepticism about the mandatory evacuation that was ordered by the city officials. People did not believe it was going to be that bad. They had ridden out storms before. Many people, whether by choice or necessity, remained behind to weather the storm. This was a decision that cost many people their lives, and untold trauma to countless others.

We lived about one hundred miles inland, but according to reports, we would be in the path of the storm. Larry was on oxygen so I knew we had to evacuate. We left on Sunday and went to Jackson, Mississippi to stay with one of Larry's cousins, Diane. I took one portable oxygen tank and his concentrator. I felt we would go home on Monday because the storm should be over by then. About two o'clock on Monday afternoon, the electricity went off at Diane's house. It was pretty rough weather, even that far inland. Now what was I going to do? The electricity stayed off and I knew I had to make a decision about what to do. Around five o'clock in the afternoon we decided to head toward home. Huge mistake! We made it okay until I turned off I-49 at Mendenhall, Mississippi.

As I began to make my way south through Prentiss, Mississippi, I practically came to a crawl. There was so much destruction and so many trees down; at times we had to wait until someone could cut a tree from the roadway. The trip is normally around three hours, but I could see it was going to be a very long and difficult drive. I thought about turning around, but I had more portable oxygen tanks at home and knew I was going to need them. Larry's tank was getting low. The closer we came to Bogalusa, the worse our travel conditions became.

We came through the little town of Angie, Louisiana and evidently a tornado had ripped through. It was dark, but I could see enough to know this was the worst destruction I had ever seen. I finally arrived in Bogalusa, and there was so much destruction I could not even recognize the streets. I could not tell where I was. It was about midnight by this time, and I was mentally and physically exhausted. I could not reach anyone on the phone to find out anything. Nothing was working! Finally, a policeman stopped me because there was a curfew in place and I was far beyond that. I explained to him how I was trying to get to my house to get some extra oxygen tanks for my husband. The policeman guided me through to the edge of town, where I felt I would be okay going forward. I thanked the officer and headed toward our subdivision.

As I turned onto the road going into our sub-division, all I could say was, "OH MY GOD!" I must have said that a dozen times as I tried to make it to our street. There were power lines down everywhere! There were trees down across the road in thirty to forty feet intervals. I had never seen anything like it. I could not believe my eyes. I could not see the houses very clearly, but I knew the damage was astounding.

I had gone to church with Diane on Sunday night and had prayed for God to protect our home since we had no insurance. Because of all the medical and work issues, we just could not afford the coverage. I was so scared to see what our house looked like. When I finally made it to our street and made it to our house, I soon discovered I could not get to the house. There were so many trees down I could only see the corners of the two story home we lived in. I saw there was no way; I could not even walk to the house. There were too many power lines down and I knew I could not make it. I managed to turn around and leave. I had no idea what to do next.

As I left the subdivision, I thought, "I'll try to make it to Sue's." Sue is my sister who lived across town. I was slowly trying to get to my sister's house, and we went down Lee's Creek Road. About a half mile down the road, I saw water ahead. As I approached the water, I could see it running across the road, but I could not tell how deep it was. Larry said, "I think you can make it through." I slowly started into the water, and very quickly realized I could not go through it! It was too deep and too swift.

"I cannot make it." I said and started backing up as quickly as I could. I had heard about other people getting swept away by currents that were too strong and I did not want that to happen to us. It took me a little while to back up to turn around. I was beyond tired and frustrated by this time, but I was trying to keep my emotions in check. I knew it would not help to panic.

I weaved and crawled through what seemed like a maze until I was on the road where my sister lived. Then, we encountered another tree down across the road and could not get to her house! There was a church on this road, so I made my way to the parking lot and told Larry, "We can stay here until morning. In another four hours it will be daylight, then we can tell more about everything." It was so hot! I would run the car for thirty minutes so we could run the air conditioner and listen to the WWL radio station in New Orleans to find out what

100

was happening. We were hearing horror stories. The devastation was unparalleled!

Now that I was stopped, my mind turned to my family that was not with me. My daughter Melissa lived in Mandeville; just across the lake from New Orleans. I knew Melissa and Baron were planning to evacuate and were probably okay. Mark and Matthew had stayed behind in Bogalusa, thinking the storm probably would not be that bad. Boy, were they wrong! There was no electricity in Bogalusa. The whole city was devastated.

When we finally saw the sun coming up it seemed impossible for so much destruction to happen in a few hours. Everything was blacked out. No phone service; you could not get in or out on your phone. You could not communicate with anyone except to travel to that person. Larry and I went back to our subdivision and it was even more horrendous in the daylight. I had to somehow manage to get inside my house and get some oxygen tanks.

I managed to make my way from the road through limbs and downed trees to the back of the house. There were about eight big pine trees down in my front yard. Three of them were lying across my driveway. There was no way to get up my driveway! There were trees down in the back of my house! There were trees down all around my house, but I noticed one amazing thing. Our house was fine. There was not one tree on it! This was another God Moment! Only God could have kept those trees off our house.

I found out later most of our neighbors had trees through their roofs. I remember speaking with one of my neighbors after the storm and telling him of how I had prayed for God to protect our house and how He did.

My neighbor's reply was, "I sure wish you had prayed for the rest of us!" I felt badly when he made that statement, but honestly, I did not pray for the whole neighborhood.

"Man, if I had known it was going to be this bad, I would have been on my knees all night!" I replied. I went to check on Mark and Matthew. Everyone was in the same situation. Everyone was very hot and trying to find somewhere to get a little ice and food. The situation was so bad in New Orleans that no one knew how bad it was in our little city. Evidently several tornadoes had come through in addition to the hurricane.

Mark was sick, went to the emergency room and was turned away. They said they had no way to help him. He was told to go home, try to stay hydrated and stay as cool as he could. I checked on as many of my family as I could, then I went back to our house to check on Larry.

After two days of no sleep and no air, I knew we could not stay at our house. I knew I had to get Larry somewhere that had electricity. He was running out of oxygen and we were miserable. I asked Matthew and Mark to come with us. We had to leave. It was too much devastation and it would be weeks, if not months before we could expect things to return to any kind of normalcy. I went to town to fill up my gas tank so we could leave and the lines were a mile to two miles long. Larry was in the car with me and I did not have much gas. I knew I would have to leave the car running to keep him cool, so when I spotted a policeman, I thought,

"He'll help me!" I drove up beside the officer, rolled down my window, and said, "Officer, is there any way that you can help me get some gas. My husband is on oxygen and I do not know if I have enough gas to sit in line and wait, because I cannot kill the car."

He looked at me and replied, "You will have to go to the back of the line like everyone else." I was pretty astounded. To myself I silently prayed, "What now, God? You know I cannot wait in line." This sounds like something made up, but as I turned and left that area, I went about a block and a man motioned for me to get in line. I was the last car they accepted, because gas was being rationed on the orders of the Washington Parish sheriff. There was only so much gas. The most amazing thing was there were only ten to twelve cars ahead of me. You could only get so much gas; you could not get as much as you wanted. People were there with gas cans and trying to get ahead to fill the cans. Thankfully, at this particular gas station, they were monitoring the purchases and not letting people get ahead of the people in line. Another God Moment!

We left Bogalusa on Thursday, and I wanted to go through Brookhaven to check on Mike. I learned that he was in a special needs shelter. Due to Mike's machines, they had to evacuate their home when the electricity went out in Brookhaven. Then, he had to be put in the hospital, since he was not able to stay at the shelter.

I was desperately trying to find somewhere to stay. I had no idea where we would go. I thought maybe there was a church in the Brookhaven area that would allow us stay for the night, and we could find a place the next day. I went by Mike and Shelia's and found out their new church had the electricity restored. Praise God! Maybe we could go there.

I went to the church with the intention of asking if we could stay for the night, but the Pastor's daughter, who was talking on the phone when I went in, hung up the phone and when I explained our plight, she said, "There is a shelter down the road." I thanked her and we headed down the road to find the shelter. The Red Cross shelter we found was an incredible place. I will never forget those wonderful Baptist people who took us into their church without hesitation. They treated us with so much dignity and provided for our every need. God definitely lead us to the right place. Thank you again, God for people that truly care about others.

Finally, in the Brookhaven area, we were able to make contact with our daughter. She was extremely relieved to discover we were being taken care of. For three days she had been agonizing about where we were and what we were experiencing. She and Baron went home after a few days and left again. It was a long and laborious process after Katrina. There were so many dead, and so many hurting.

My son, Mark, never joined us in Brookhaven and I did not know what happened. I could not talk to anyone, so I had to trust God to take care of him. I knew he was sick and I was terribly worried after he never came to join us. I found out later he had made it to McComb, Mississippi, but had to sleep in his truck. He too, was experiencing difficulty getting gas so he decided to turn around and go back to Bogalusa. His decision almost cost him his life.

We were okay in the shelter, but Mike was having

serious problems. Since he had to be admitted to the hospital, hospice care was dismissed. That is the way they do it. You cannot be on hospice and go to a hospital. When Mike was released from the hospital, he was put in another special needs shelter. After a period of time, they were going to close the shelter and there was nowhere for Mike to stay. His hospice nurse, Nona, made the decision that she wanted to take Mike into her home and take care of him until he could return home. Wow! Another God Moment!

Nurses are taught not to get emotionally attached to their patients, but Nona is not your average nurse. In fact, she won the "Hero of the Year" award the McComb Enterprise Journal gives each year after they learned of her incredible act of kindness. She probably saved Mike's life. I will never forget this wonderful, dedicated woman who took care of my son's needs during this very trying and painful time in our life. I think he was in her home for about two weeks until his electricity returned. Thanks again, Nona!

The storm occurred on August 29th, 2005 and we did not get electricity in my subdivision until early October. I was so desperate when I returned to Bogalusa. The shelter was going to close soon, so we made our way home. Most of the city had electricity, but most of the outlying areas were still struggling with the heat and trying to be patient, knowing that the crews were working tirelessly to try to restore power.

I finally stopped a big power truck and explained to him that my husband was sick and how badly I needed electricity. This wonderful man came directly to our home and worked until we had power. Unlike the policeman who was so unfeeling, this sweet man went out of his way to help us. There were power trucks from all over the country, as far away as Ohio that had come to our town to help. You find out what people are like in a time of crisis, and there are some places and people that will be forever in my heart for their gracious and kind deeds. Others will be there for the opposite reason.

"O Lord our Lord, how excellent is thy name in all the earth! Who hast set thy glory above the heavens."

Psalm 8:1

Chapter 14

Losing the Game

Larry Smith
Southwest Mississippi Community College 1966

The stress of almost losing Mike, Mark and Larry during Katrina was over whelming. I was still reeling from the day to day stress of having four close family members with a debilitating disease. Larry was never a complainer and I know many times he suffered in silence. He knew my heart was heavy seeing Mike suffer daily.

Larry had two bad falls; one during some tests at a hospital and another at our house. He was pretty much immobile and had to use a power chair to get around now. He had stopped working and had accepted his disability. Only six weeks after Katrina, he became very sick and had to be hospitalized. At first the doctors thought it was his gall bladder, but it was finally determined he had pancreatitis.

Dr. Morrison, Larry's doctor, whose mom had suffered with Muscular Dystrophy, was familiar with the needs of MD patients. She took me aside, talked to me and told me Larry would probably never leave the hospital. I was not expecting to hear this grim prognosis. She explained to me how hard it is for a healthy person to overcome this condition, so it would be virtually impossible for Larry. He was too weak and his lungs kept getting worse. He developed pneumonia and battled for three weeks. He wanted to live, and it was so heart-wrenching for me to watch my basketball player lose his game. He was a fighter, but this was one fight he could not win.

We had the most amazing thing happen a few hours before Larry passed from this life. The family had been called in and Jerry, Larry's brother, had brought Mom to see him. We decided to take the big bubble mask off for a few moments. God gave us some sweet moments with Larry as he sang "Poor Old Kaw-Lija" and entertained us with his humor. Mom had been through so much, having lost two of her four children, and now facing losing the third child. Muscular Dystrophy was taking a heavy toll in the Smith Family.

There is always so much to deal with after you lose someone close to you. After Mike's accident in 1998, five months later we lost Helen, Larry's sister. She had been in the hospital with some heart issues, but she came home and a couple of days later she got up and fell over. Her heart just stopped! In May 2001, Larry's brother, Glen, went into the hospital to have knee surgery. He came home the next morning and died the next day. Two years later, Dad passed away in May 2003. Then on December 5, 2005, Larry passed away. The horrific disease of Muscular Dystrophy was killing off the Smith family at an alarming rate.

After Larry died, I had the task of deciding what to do about our home. I knew the house was too big for me, even though I loved our home. I knew I needed to put it on the market and sell to downsize. I had enough equity that I could purchase something else and not have a house note. I called a realtor and put it on the market in 2006. One night as I was lying in bed, I prayed, "God, please send a buyer for the house." A very short and simple prayer. The house was on the market only a couple of weeks when a man from Washington saw it listed. He sent an agent to check it out and he bought the house without even coming to see it. One more God Moment Miracle!

When we went to close the sale, after everything was transacted, the new buyer called me aside and asked, "What are your plans?" I told him I was not sure, I would probably live with my daughter for a little while until I found something else to buy. He looked at me and said, "I have to stay in Washington for two more years and if you would like to stay in your home, I would be glad to have you there." I think someone had told this nice man some of our circumstances and he felt compassion.

I replied, "That is incredibly sweet of you to make an offer like that but I will have to talk to my daughter, and give it some thought. Thank you so much, though!" After thinking about his generous offer, I decided I would not feel at home there any more, knowing someone else owned it. I declined his offer, graciously, I hope.

God blessed me so much in allowing the house to sell quickly. There were so many things I needed to do. So many times, I would go to Mike's and often I would say, "Baby, is there anything I can do for you, do you need anything?"

"Well since you asked, you could bring me a sack full of money." He had that little grin on his face when he said it. I knew the struggles he and Shelia dealt with on a daily basis. I knew even though he was joking, he really could use a sack full of money. Trying to raise two children with very little money was exhausting, mentally and emotionally.

After the sale of my house, I gave each of my children ten thousand dollars. Since Mike had made the statement to me about a sack full of money, I decided to put his ten thousand dollars in a paper bag and surprise him. He had no idea I was going to do this. I got the whole ten thousand in one dollar bills, so it would seem like a lot of money. I will never forget the look on Mike's face when I went in and handed him a paper bag. He looked at me and said, "What's this?"

I smiled as I handed him the bag and said, "It's a little present for you."

He took the paper bag and opened it and looked inside. The tears started rolling down his cheeks, and I could not hold mine back either! "You are always asking for a sack of money, so I thought I would bring you one." I said. I wish it could have been more. It truly blessed them, making a way for Shelia to have another vehicle and the ability to pay a few bills. That was truly a God Moment!

After Larry's passing, I stayed with my wonderful daughter, Melissa and her loving husband, Baron. They welcomed me into their home. My sweet daughter wanted to shield me from anything that could hurt me. She is still very protective of her mom. I know now why God insisted I have another child. He knew how much I was going to need her. My daughter is a very special woman of faith and I respect her walk with God. I called upon her many times during Mike's and Larry's sickness. We have had a few times we did not see eye to eye, but we both have strong personalities. I would not change a thing about my daughter.

Her paternal grandmother loved to make her frilly dresses. Since this was our only daughter, after three boys, there was no way she was going to be a tomboy. I adored having a little girl to primp and frill. She may not have enjoyed it, but her Nanny and I sure did. Mom would go into a children's clothing store, come home and duplicate the most beautiful little dresses. I hardly ever bought clothes for Melissa. Mom enjoyed sewing, and I enjoyed letting her. She was a very accomplished seamstress, so anything that she made was top quality. Mom always said that Melissa had a bubbly personality, and this is true. She displays a joyful spirit and makes friends wherever she goes.

Then I started in earnest searching for a house to buy. I knew my sweet daughter would let me stay with her, but you know what they say about mother-in-laws.

I thought I might wear my welcome out with my sweet son-in-law and I definitely did not want to do that. He is precious and I feel that he loves me. I wanted it to stay that way.

One day while I was in Bogalusa, I passed a house which belonged to my sister's mother-in-law, who had passed away. The house had been vacant for some time. My sister told me when I asked about it, "Ann, Debbie and Terry have wanted to buy that place for a long time, but Vicki will not sell it." The house had some Katrina damage. God impressed me this was the house he wanted me to have. I asked my sister, Sue, for Vicki's telephone number and decided I did not have anything to lose by calling and asking. I was totally shocked when Vicki said, "We have just been discussing what we were going to do with that property. As soon as my husband gets back, we will give you a call." I was surprised she did not give me a "No" answer.

They did return my call and to make a long story short, I bought the house. I had to put a little money into it, but I was very happy with the price and within a short time I moved into my new home. Thanks again, God! What would I do without the Master? When you live for God, He really does move on people and in situations to change things. I truly believe this. Everything is not just happenstance. God Moment Miracles happen in our lives more often than most of us stop to recognize.

"But as it is written, Eye hath not seen, nor ear heard, neither have entered into the heart of man, the things which God hath prepared for them that love him."

1 Corinthians 2:9

Desmond's: Melissa's Family
Amy, Mark, Baron, Melissa, Seth, Alissa

Chapter 15

A Missing Child

Melissa and Baron have three children, and I must share a story of how Alissa was named. You would think it was after her Mom, but this is how it happened. Baron and Melissa could not decide on a name for their baby girl. I do not know who came up with this idea, but it was a good one. For the last month of Melissa's pregnancy, they filled in names of the baby on their calendar. Melissa picked out a few and Baron had his choices, so for each day they alternated writing in a name on the calendar. The date the baby was born would determine the name choice. They slotted in names a full month ahead of the birth. Wow, what a way to name a child! I wish I had a list of all the names because there were some strange ones. Melissa had given Mark Scott the privilege of giving his little sister her middle name. Whatever date the birthdate was, would determine the first name and Mark Scott would pick her middle name. It happened she was born on August 4, and the name was Alissa. Mark had chosen Gabriella as his choice for the middle name. Therefore, her name is Alissa Gabriella Desmond. Beautiful! God was definitely in on this one.

Once when I was babysitting for Melissa, Alissa was around four years old, I had a very scary event happen. Larry was with me, and he was pretty advanced in his illness at this time. I put the two little ones to bed and Mark had to take some movies back to the rental store. I put the children to bed and asked Larry to listen out for the children while I drove Mark to return the movies. The trip was around fifteen to twenty minutes, so I was not concerned that it might be unsafe. I felt the children would be asleep when I returned. I entered the house and immediately went in to make sure Alissa and Seth were asleep. Alissa was not in her bed. I went into the living room where Larry was sitting and asked him, "Honey, where is Alissa?"

"I do not know, she should be in her bed." He replied.

.   "She is not there." I said. "Did she come in here while I was gone?" I went back throughout the house looking for her. She was nowhere in sight. I was beginning to feel panic. I thought, "Larry must have fallen asleep." We rushed into the back yard to see if

116

she was there. She was not. I sent Mark to the neighbor's house, thinking she might have gone there. They all came back to see what was going on. I was in serious panic mode by this time.

I called 911 and told them I had a missing child. Right after I called 911, someone shouted, "Here she is!" I rushed to see, and sure enough, there she was. She was under the covers in her mom's bed. She was completely covered up and looked like a pillow. She was sound asleep. The commotion woke her and we were all so glad she was okay. The police arrived, but thank God, we did not need them; they were also glad we did not need them.

I told Melissa what happened when she called to check on the children. She laughingly said, "Mom, it looks like I am going to have to get another baby sitter." Every time I hear or read something about a child missing, I think about how quickly a child can disappear. You do not give it much thought until you are faced with a situation. Then you understand.

There was another time in July 2006 that Melissa and Baron had taken a trip to Hawaii and I was keeping the children. Melissa hired a young girl named Amber to help me, so I felt everything would be fine. One day around lunchtime, I decided to take the children to McDonald's for lunch.

It was a hot day and we started to get into the van. I went to the passenger side of the van to buckle Alissa into her car seat while Amber buckled Seth into his seat on the other side. As I was about to fasten the car seat, without thinking, I tossed the keys to the van into the front passenger seat. I closed the door of the van and immediately heard the click of the locks as the van locked! Oh, no! I thought. It never occurred to me the van locked automatically when the doors closed.

I knew I had to think quickly, because in a matter of minutes, the temperature in the van would be elevating. I told Amber to go ask Mark Scott if he knew of another set of keys anywhere in the house. She ran to check. There were no extra keys, so I decided to call a locksmith to see how quickly they could arrive. I told Amber to stay with the children and try to keep them calm. I rushed inside to call the locksmith. He informed me it would be about twenty minutes before he could arrive. I pleaded with him to get there as quickly as he could.

I ran back outside to check on the kids. They had started to get upset and hot since no one else was getting into the van. The children had no idea what was happening. I ran back inside and called 911 and explained the situation. The lady wanted to keep me on the phone, but I told her I could not stay on the phone, I had to go see about the children. I told her to get someone there as soon as she could.

When I went back outside, the children were crying and beginning to sweat. I tried to calm them but there was no way to do that. I was in full panic mode and kept thinking, "Come on! Where are you?" For some strange reason, the idea of breaking a window did not enter my mind. Later, as I thought back on the situation, breaking a window should have been the first thing I did, but I was not thinking clearly at all.

I was standing on one side of the van and Amber was on the other, and we were trying to talk to the children and calm them. The more they cried, the hotter they became. The situation was not good at all. Amber's mom drove up and Mark Scott was still in bed; not knowing what was going on outside. Why didn't someone suggest I break a window? No one said anything! We were all in panic mode and the children were in grave danger. I could see Alissa beginning to want to go to sleep and I was terrified. I knew time was rapidly running out!

A full fifteen minutes passed before the police car pulled into the driveway. The policeman had the car door open within a moment. We grabbed the children and ran into the house with them to get them cooled down. Their little faces were red and they were drenched with sweat! We wet some cloths and began to wipe their faces and get them cooled down. We gave them some water to get them hydrated. I had heard horror stories of children being left in vehicles, but I never dreamed I would be dealing with a situation like this. I could not bring myself to tell Melissa of the near tragedy that occurred. I knew if I did, it would spoil the rest of her vacation.

When you are faced with something like this, you think you would be calm and think clearly, but sometimes you do not. Nobody said, "Why don't you break the window?" The people around me did not suggest it and I wish someone had. Everything turned out okay, but what if it had not? How would I have been able to cope if something had happened to two of the most precious people in my life? I think God knew I could not have handled it. Thanks again, God. It seems that rescuing me keeps You busy!

One of my favorite things to do is be with my grandchildren. I love them so much. There is nothing I would not do to help one of them. I think they love me with a very special love, also. I have this little ritual I do for them on their birthdays. I will get little gifts for months ahead of time and wrap them. When their birthday arrives, I have collected a pile of gifts. They enjoy opening a lot of gifts and I enjoy it as much as they do.

Chapter 16

The Need to Pray

One morning as I was riding in my car, I felt a strong urge to pray for Matthew. I called Melissa and said, "I do not know what is going on with Matt, but I feel very strongly that he needs prayer. Please go to prayer for him." Melissa assured me she would and I began to pray also. This was around ten o'clock in the morning. I tried to call Matt to see what was going on but got no answer. Later that day, my phone rang and it was Matt. "I called to let you know that I had a wreck." he said.

"Are you hurt, son?" was my first response.

"No, we are okay, but God really had his hand on us this morning. We got hit by an eighteen wheeler in Tylertown. The policeman could not believe we walked away from it without even having to go to the hospital. He said we were very lucky. I knew we were incredibly blessed!" He went on to explain the four-way stop had been changed to a red light and he thought it was still a four-way stop. He had the red light, but he thought the other lane also had a red light. The wreck happened around eleven o'clock in the morning. God was warning me about that wreck!

When I went to take some pictures of the truck, there was no doubt in my mind a miracle had taken place that morning. The front of the truck was totaled and the back glass of the truck was shattered. Amazingly, the front glass and both side windows were completely intact. It looked as though God had placed His hand around them in that front seat. Matthew had his wife, Marilyn, and his step-grandchild in the truck, and none of them had their seat belts on. Thanks again, God! You are so mindful of what we need!

Just a few months later, in November 2006, Matthew was going to take a guy home from work and he was driving at night in unfamiliar territory. It was around ten o'clock at night and again the phone rings. I do not remember who called, but Matthew had been involved in another accident! They treated him at Bogalusa Medical Center and transferred him to Slidell Memorial Hospital which was a bigger and better equipped hospital. I know when they are transferring, it is not a good sign. I immediately left for the Slidell Hospital and upon arriving, discovered he had some cuts to his face and was pretty banged up. His oxygen saturation was low and he was administered oxygen. He had some internal injuries with bleeding through his kidneys. I picked glass from his eyelashes. That is how close glass came to getting into his eyes.

He began to relate to me how the wreck happened and I felt so sorry for what he had been through. He said he was going about 55 mph and all of a sudden, there was no road, just a ditch. He went into the woods about fifty feet. The truck hit a tree and flipped onto the driver's side. This truck was a small Chevrolet S-10 and with his right leg being unable to bend, he did not know how he was going to get out of the truck. He was bleeding from his facial cuts. He said his Bible was there on the seat beside him. He prayed! A God Moment Miracle!

He managed to climb out of the truck through the back window. Considering how small the window was, I was amazed he got through that opening. He found himself in the back of the truck and managed to climb out onto the ground. He could not walk at all. He knew he had to get back to the road to get some help, but because of the limbs and it being at night, he had to scoot and crawl to the road. He did not have a cell phone to call anyone, so he managed to pull himself up and make it across the road to a house.

The few cars that came by kept on going. He saw some lights on in a house across the road and managed to get to the house and get help. The people inside the house would not open the door but did call 911 and summoned help. When the police arrived, the first thing they wanted to know was if Matthew had been drinking. I guess that is procedure, but Matthew quickly informed them he did not drink. He was transported to the hospital and then transferred to Slidell.

When I went to the facility where his truck was towed to take some pictures, the man that owned the place said, "I hesitate to ask, but is the person that was in this truck alive?"

"Yes, he is and it looks as if he is going to be okay." I replied.

The man shook his head and said, "When I went to pick up this vehicle, I would not have believed anyone could have survived! He hit a tree eight feet off the ground and it was about fifty feet into the woods. I saw the bark torn off the tree. If he made it, you can say you have been given one miracle."

"Matthew is a walking miracle anyway. God has had his hand on his life for a long time and this is not his first miracle." I said.

God so beautifully made a way for Matthew and Marilyn to be able to buy a nice home and because of his disabilities, he qualified for a one percent loan. He was so proud of his new home and had only lived there about six months when he learned of his wife's infidelity. He was heartbroken and tried to make everything work out, but evidently her heart was somewhere else. The guy Marilyn chose was someone who Matthew and Marilyn had taken in off the streets. He was living in their home. After confronting his wife and hearing her confession, Matthew told both of them to leave. Matthew heard the words, "I'll be back!" from the stranger he had befriended.

I got a call from Matthew late one night, "Mom, there is a chair on fire in my living room!" I had been there that day cleaning and the living room was clean. There was nothing that should have caused a fire. It was summertime and there were no heaters or anything to start a fire. Matthew did not smoke, so I knew it was not from a cigarette.

"Son, call the fire department!" were my next words.

"I already have. I am standing outside in my underwear." He stated. The fire trucks arrived, so Matthew had to get off the phone. I called my sister, Shelia, and told her to go check on the situation since I lived twenty miles away.

"Ann, it's more than just a chair on fire, his house is burning!" Shelia stated a few minutes later when she called me.

Matthew was very upset, but as I talked to him the next morning, he told me, "Mom, as I was standing there watching my house burn, God gave me this scripture. I Thessalonians 5:18: "In everything give thanks: for this is the will of God in Christ Jesus concerning you." Wow! How can you wrap your mind around that? God is telling you that it is His will. The fire alarm was outside Matthew's bedroom and if he had waited another minute, he probably would not have been able to get out. He could not exit through the front door and the kitchen door would have been cut off in a matter of minutes. He barely made it out in time.

The fire Marshall ruled it an electrical fire, but because of where the fire started, there was no way this could have been an electrical fire. The ruling proved to be a blessing because the insurance company did not hesitate to pay. I later found the bottom portion of an aluminum ball bat. It was in the rubble where the chair was. Since I had cleaned that day, I knew this was an item that was not in the room before the fire.

Sometimes God takes evil and turns it for good. I thought the insurance was in both of their names, but it turned out that it was only in Matthew's name. I had furnished the house for them, so there was nothing in the house belonging to Marilynn, except her clothes. I had given them a beautiful pecan dining room set which had been my husband's and my first major purchase after we got married. This was a cherished heirloom and I was so sorry to see it burned.

Only God knows whether this tragedy was an accident or intentional, but to think that someone would attempt to harm one of the most giving and loving people on Earth, made me mad. God keeps good records, though, and I know eventually, justice will come.

In mid-2008, my son Matthew, needed gall bladder surgery. I talked to the doctor and told her he was a MMD patient. I requested a consult with anesthesia, but was still concerned. I had learned even the simplest of medical events can become major with no warning. The surgery should have been about thirty minutes. I was anxiously awaiting news that everything had gone as planned. After an hour and having heard nothing, I began to get worried. After another thirty minutes, I went to the desk and inquired about Matthew's condition. The attendant said she would check on him and let me know. She called surgery and was told they were having some problems with him. I became frantic! I paced the floor for another thirty minutes and began to call people to ask them to pray. Finally, the doctor came out and called me into a little room close to the waiting area.

She sat down and said, "You tried to tell me. This is the worst case I have ever experienced. He is still not out of the woods."

"What happened?" I asked.

"He is having trouble with hypothermia. This is the first time I have experienced this." the doctor said.

"With a MMD patient, anything can happen. I have learned that." I replied. I remembered when Larry had to have surgery on his wrist and on his knee. They refused to put him to sleep so they did a block. It is dangerous to put a MMD patient to sleep. Matthew pulled out of it and was okay, but it gave the doctor and me a real scare.

The good news is, I think the disease ends with my children. Mark has one child and he does not have any symptoms. Matthew has no children and Mike's children, Whitney and Michael, have hopefully escaped this disease. Michael is scheduled to go to MDA in New Orleans in a couple of months to be checked. Whitney has not been tested, but shows no signs. I am praying for God's mercy; that Whitney and Michael will be spared the agony of this debilitating disease.

When Matthew was in his twenties, he dated a young lady named Donna Kelly. These two truly loved each other, but Donna had a bad experience with a guy she dated and was very hesitant to say yes to Matthew's proposal of marriage. Matthew felt if Donna really loved him, she would marry him, so he broke up with her. He married the first person that came along after that. The marriage lasted ten years, but I watched as time after time Matthew was mistreated by Marilynn. Matthew worked two jobs to try to make her happy. They were just part-time, but he was doing the best he could.

After his house burned and he had a divorce, one day he decided to contact Donna. He really did not know what was going on in her life, but after his phone call, he found out she was still single. They reconnected and were married in a beautiful ceremony in November, 2008. I could not believe Donna had waited for ten years for the love of her life. How amazing. Yes, I could believe it. A God Moment Miracle!

> **"Who comforteth us in all our tribulation, that we may be able to comfort them which are in any trouble, by the comfort wherewith we ourselves are comforted of God."**
> *II Corinthians 1:4*

Chapter 17

Not Me, God!

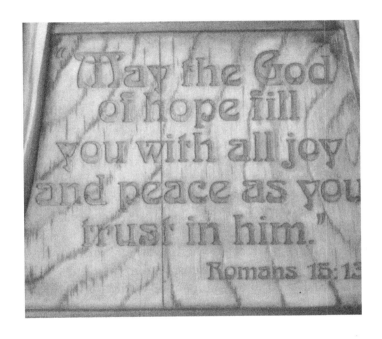

In 2007, we lost my sweet mother-in-law, Johnnie Mae Smith. This woman took me under her wing as her daughter-in-law and taught me so much. Larry and I lived in their home for a time and Mom taught me to cook and sew, not with the expertise she had, but it was so much fun to learn to make clothes. I never felt anything but love from Mom and Dad and they were such a wonderful part of my life. Toward the end of their lives, Larry and I had the privilege of caring for them for a little while. Dad got sick and after he was discharged from the hospital, mom decided the nursing home was the appropriate place for Dad to get the constant care he needed. He died after a few months there. He was ninety-two, so God had blessed him with a long life.

Mom was lost after dad died. She was staying with us and one day she told us she wanted to go to the nursing home. We tried to talk her out of it, but to no avail. She had made up her mind. I think she felt we had too much on our plate. She knew we were dealing with Mike's sickness and with her sweet and kind spirit, she did not want to be a bother. We could not convince her to stay.

She was content in the nursing home for a few years before God called her home. She had lost her husband and three of her four children, but she developed Alzheimer's disease and many things left her mind. She lived in the moment or would go way back in time, but the tragic events of recent years were dim or nonexistent, which was a blessing.

It hurt her heart so much each time she had to say good-bye to one of her children. Jerry, Larry's younger brother, and I decided when Larry passed, Mom was not in a condition to come to his funeral. We felt for her health's sake, it would be better for her not to know. I had styled Mom's hair many times and when she passed, I felt I owed it to her to do her hair one last time. I had never fixed anyone's hair who was deceased, but I had to try. My sweet daughter Melissa went with me and God gave me strength to fix her hair.

As her sister was viewing mom she asked, "Who fixed Johnnie Mae's hair?" Her daughter told her I had and she came up to me and said, "When I go, will you do my hair?"

"Of course I will, Aunt Lessie, if you want me to." I replied.

I had to accept my disability with spinal problems in 2002, but God blessed me and I was able to be there for Mike and Larry. I was able to be pretty mobile, with only occasional bouts with my back. Then, one day I could not walk. The pain was so excruciating I could do nothing. I was under the care of a neurologist. After x-rays and a MRI, it was determined that I needed surgery. A disc was pressing on a nerve and I was losing the feeling in my right leg. I battled this for six weeks, taking all the pain medication I could take. I could not even turn over in bed.

I did not need to be sick. Mike needed me. Larry was gone. My family needed me. I was scheduled for surgery and was dreading it, but I knew I could not go on in my current condition. I had been healthy all my life, for which I was grateful, but whatever was going on now had to be treated.

I was reclining in a chair one Thursday when my phone rang. It was a very sweet friend, Sister Marcelli, whom I had not heard from in some time. Her first words were, "How are you doing, I haven't heard from you in a while and I was thinking about you."

"Sis, I am not doing well at all." I replied. "In fact, I am on a lot of pain medication and I am scheduled for surgery on Tuesday."

"I am going to get my husband on the phone and we

are going to pray for you right now." she said. I welcomed anything that could help and knowing this prayer warrior as I did, I was delighted to have her and Brother Marcelli pray for me. They are both ministers and have awesome faith. They prayed and we talked a little more and then we hung up the phone with the assurance they would keep me in their prayers. I did not realize it at the moment, but God healed me.

Nothing spectacular happened. I did not feel any different until later that day. I realized I was not hurting nearly as badly as I had been. I still did not realize I was healed. I was just thankful I was not in so much pain.

The next morning, which was a Friday, I felt much better. I could move around and the pain was gone. I still did not realize I was healed. I knew I felt a lot better. By the next day, Saturday, I was feeling really good. I was in no pain so I called my daughter and said, "Melissa, I am so much better. If I am feeling this good tomorrow, I am coming to church."

"Mom, you take care of yourself, don't over exert." was her reply. On Sunday morning, I felt awesome so I got dressed and went to church. The feeling had returned to my right leg, and the fact I could walk was amazing.

"God has healed me!" I told my daughter. I realized that something miraculous had happened. "If I am feeling this good tomorrow, I am not having surgery." She was a little skeptical about me canceling my surgery. She had seen how bad things could get with my back. She had to get me to the hospital once when I could not get off the couch. I was in the hospital for a few days that time.

On Monday morning, I knew I was not going to have the surgery. I felt too good. I called and cancelled the surgery. On Wednesday after I had cancelled, I was in a prayer meeting when I got a call from my doctor's nurse, "Miss Barbara, the doctor wants to know if you can come in to see him."

"Sure," I replied, "I will be right there." I left the meeting and headed to the doctor's office. I fully intended to tell him I was healed, but when I got in his office, he immediately pulled out my MRI and x-rays and began by saying, "I really do not want to scare you, but I need to let you know if you do not have this surgery, you stand a good chance of losing the use of your leg permanently." He showed me on the x-ray where the nerve root was being compressed.

"Well, doctor, if you feel that strongly about it, I will get back on the surgery schedule." I left his office after telling Jackie, his nurse, to put me back on the surgery schedule.

"Okay, Miss Barbara, I will call you tomorrow." Jackie told me.

On the way home, I said, "God, I know you have touched my body. If this surgery is not your will, please block it." I prayed this prayer in my mind and did not think anything more about it. Jackie was supposed to call me the next day, but late in the afternoon, she had not called, so I called her. "Jackie, you got me on the schedule yet?" I asked.

"No, Miss Barbara, I'll call you tomorrow," she said. This was on Friday and again I waited all day for her to call. By late afternoon, she still had not called, so again, I called her.

"Jackie, do you have me back on the schedule?" I asked the second time.

"No, Miss Barbara, I'll get with you on Monday." she replied. As soon as I hung up the phone, a little light went off in my brain. "You asked me to block it," this voice said in my mind. "Okay, God, I get it! I will not call back." I told myself. If she does not call me, I am going to accept that you do not want me to have this surgery. I did not call and she never called me.

The next Wednesday, the exact same thing happened. I was in a prayer meeting, again my phone rang, and again it was the nurse calling. I went immediately to the doctor's office, but this time I had made up my mind. God had shown me it was not his will for me to have surgery. I walked into the doctor's office and before he had a chance to say anything, I said, "Doctor, I am not having surgery. I am not in pain, I have the feeling back in my leg, and as long as I feel this good, I am not having surgery! I had two wonderful preachers pray for me and I feel God has touched my body."

He reached out, took my hand and covered it with both of his. "Let me check that leg," he said.
He examined it and he kind of exhaled and said, "This is really unusual."

"Doctor, I may have to call you and beg you to operate on me at some point, but as long as I feel this good, I cannot have surgery." I told him. He was okay with that. I left his office with so much gratitude in my heart. I do not know why God chose to heal me, but I am thankful He did. I went around telling everyone who would listen what God had done for me!

134

That has been five years ago and I am still healed. I wanted to know by way of an MRI that God had done the work that needed to be done. I went to a different doctor, and with my history, I had no problem getting him to do an MRI. I have the evidence to prove that when God does something, He does it well. I may have problems in the next five minutes, but it will be a different problem than I had. I am not immune to health problems, so I do not want anyone to misunderstand, but I will always give Almighty God the credit for healing my spine. Another God Moment Miracle!

> "To everything there is a season,
> And a time to every purpose
> Under the heaven."
>
> *Ecclesiastes 3:1*

Chapter 18

It's Time

At this time, in 2007, Mike's disease was progressing rapidly, and I knew that he was not going to be here much longer. Shelia and Mike had moved from Brookhaven back to Jayess, Mississippi so Shelia could be close to her family for Mike's final days. I was happy to see them make this move because it was closer for me to travel to be with Mike. He treasured my visits and I did too. Every moment I could spend with my precious son was indeed special.

We both knew his time was swiftly drawing near. He was not afraid of dying. He loved his children so much and wanted to be with them as long as God would allow. He was able to be here for his daughter's prom and see her in her beautiful gown. Whitney was his firstborn and he loved her so much, and she loved her Dad tremendously. Whitney was there for Mike. She would wait on him and do anything to make him more comfortable.

He loved his son, Michael, just as much. It hurt him that he was never able to play ball with him, go camping or do any of the things that a dad usually does with his son. Michael was only seven when his dad first came home from the hospital, so most of his childhood memories are not good ones. I am sure to Michael it seemed like living in a hospital. That was pretty much what their home had become in order to have Mike at home.

In December 2007, it was getting close to Christmas and I always have a family celebration with all the kids; gift giving and cooking seafood gumbo. This was a celebration Mike always enjoyed so much. Shelia told me Mike wanted to come to my house for the celebration. Since I had remarried, I knew he wanted to come see where I lived and make sure in his own mind that I was okay. Shelia and I knew he should not make this trip, but Mike was insistent. We all knew this would be his last Christmas so we did everything we could to fulfill his every wish. He was so weak Shelia had to tie his head to the back of the seat to keep it upright, but he came.

We had an awesome time, but I knew it was taking every ounce of strength Mike had just to be here. As much as he loved gumbo, he barely ate any. We put the Santa hat on him and let him give out the presents to the kids. He enjoyed it so much and we did too, but it was taking a toll on his strength. He could not stay long, but he accomplished his goal. He saw where I lived and he got to be with his family for one last time.

About a week later, while I was in church, I felt I should go up to the front of the church and have my pastor anoint me with oil and say the twenty third psalm over me. I told him I wanted to take it to Mike. I did that. I told Mike what I was impressed to do and he welcomed the anointing and the reading of the twenty third psalm over him. I did not realize the significance of this until the day that Mike went to glory.

On the day Mike was called home, I went to see him that morning and I went to his bedside and told him that I loved him. He was very weak and could not talk but mouthed the words, "I love you too." I noticed he kept lifting his hand and it would fall back by his side. I recognize now he was trying to say something and could not. I did not know it at the time.

Melissa had come and brought the children to see Mike. We knew he was very weak. His mind was alert but his body was not able to sustain life anymore. He was losing the battle!

About four o'clock in the afternoon, I went to the head of Mike's bed and I began to say words of comfort to him. I reassured him I would help take care of his children, not to worry about them, that they would be alright. I was soothing his forehead with my hand while comforting him with words God was giving me. I had not planned this nor did I know at this time God was calling him home. After being there for a while, I realized God was preparing his exit from this life.

God gave me an amazing strength at this point. Mike's brother-in-law had come in and I moved from the head of the bed to allow Chris to go say something to him. I immediately went to the bedroom and called Melissa. I told her to find somewhere to pray and to ask God to send the angels to get Mike. She assured me she would and I hung up the phone and went back to the head of Mike's bed.

As I arrived there, the Lord impressed me to sing "Coming Home", and I began to sing. As I began to sing softly, one by one, family members joined in the chorus and soon the bed was surrounded by Mike's family, singing that old hymn. I felt the awesome presence of God in such a powerful way! There was a holy presence in the room that my husband later described to me as so powerful it made the hair stand up on his arms.

In that awesome atmosphere, Mike exited this world. I know there were angels in the room! We could all feel them. I was in such awe of what just happened; there was no sadness in me. I felt a peace and a joy that I cannot even describe. My God had just given me another miracle! After nine long years on a ventilator, my baby was free. He was healed. He was with almighty God. He was not suffering anymore! I have no doubt that I will see my sweet Mike again.

Later as I talked to my daughter, she told me that

after I asked her to pray, she had gone to her bedroom, got her Bible and knelt beside her bed. She opened her Bible to the twenty-third psalm and began to pray, "The Lord is Mike's Shepherd, Mike shall not want. Mike shall lie down in green pastures. She went through the entire twenty-third psalm putting Mike's name in the verses. She told me when she had finished praying the twenty-third Psalm, she took her very long hair down and laid it across her Bible. She looked up toward heaven and said, "Lord, I have prayed many prayers for my brother, but I am invoking the power with the angles! I am asking you to send the angels right now to get my brother!"

I cried when she told me this because that is exactly what happened. God did send those angels to get Mike! The twenty-third psalm and the anointing oil all make perfect sense now. It was God's plan and timing. How mindful is our God of where we are. I have witnessed many times and told what God did. I want to share this with as many as will listen, because, if we just trust him, God will take care of His children! I miss my sweet and humble son, and I want to see him, but I would not call him back in the sick condition he was in. One day, when I do see him again, he will be dancing on the streets of gold. Mortality will have changed to immortality. Eternity will have begun!

On the one year anniversary of Mike's passing, our pastor had no idea it would have special significance for me, but he preached from the twenty-third psalm. I mentioned this to him after church that it was the anniversary of Mike's passing, and he exclaimed, "Oh, no, I did not realize this was the day." The same thing happened on the second anniversary, only by a visiting preacher who knew nothing about me or my family. On the second time this happened, I just smiled. I felt this was God's way of giving me comfort about my precious son. The third year, I was waiting, and sure enough, it happened. Not on the very day, but within a couple of days of the anniversary. On Wednesday night, January 22, 2014, I attended our regular Wednesday night church service. The singing ended and as I sat down, I glanced at my phone and saw the date. It dawned on me that it was only four days till the sixth anniversary of Mike's death. In my mind, I wondered if God was going to show up in the same manner. The service continued and about half-way through the service, completely out of context with the theme of the message, our pastor was visibly anointed as he suddenly said, "The Lord is My Shepherd, I Shall Not Want!" He had the congregation recite this passage of scripture after him. Then he said, "This is for someone." There was no doubt in my heart who it was for. I was so amazed! I knew in my heart that God had done it again! Just to confirm my thoughts, after church I approached Pastor Garcia and asked him, "I have to ask you this, was Psalms part of your scripture plan for tonight?"

He looked at me and replied, "No, it was not!" He continued, "As soon as I said it, I thought of you."

Maybe this is coincidence; or maybe not. I choose to believe that God is so mindful of where we are, he sends us little things to let us know that he is always there!

Sometimes, I get pretty overwhelmed with having so much sickness and disease in my family. Not only did my husband and three of my four children have to battle with Myotonic Muscular Dystrophy, but since my husband lost his sister, Helen, there is no one to care for her daughter and her granddaughter, who both suffer from this horrific disease. Gretchen and Elana have Myotonic Muscular Dystrophy and Gretchen is in an advanced stage. She is swiftly getting to the point she cannot go anywhere. Her mobility is very impaired.

Through the grace of God, I managed to get her some help at home or she would be in a nursing home now. Elana is congenital MD, and has been symptomatic since birth. She is twenty seven now and has mobility and mental impairment. She requires a lot of care as well as her mom. I pray daily that God will continue to give me strength to help with all my sick family.

"I have fought a good fight, I have finished my course, I have kept the faith."

2 Timothy 4:7

Chapter 19

The Unexpected

Mark Smith

When living and dealing with so much sickness, the unexpected becomes the expected. This chapter demonstrates a very different way this debilitating disease of MMD can suddenly change or claim a life. While my oldest son, Mike, struggled for a very long time after his wreck, my second son, Mark, seemed to be able to deal with his life differently. Mark shared his health condition with his boss and told him if he became unable to perform his duties, he would quit. He did not get that opportunity. He was fired! Mark had to file for and accept his total disability in 1999.

For Mark to get fired even though he could still do his job was shocking to us, and I was certain his boss could not do that. After all, wasn't there the American with Disability Act that prevented employers from this type of injustice? I do not know how I came into contact with a lawyer in New Orleans, Louisiana, but she was a corporate lawyer who was as convinced as I that a grave injustice had occurred. She took Mark's case pro-bono and went all the way to the Supreme Court, but to no avail. In the end, we had to accept the final ruling. Mark was thirty-two years old and had to file for permanent disability.

God has an amazing way of sending justice. Even though we did not pray or wish anything bad for this company, which was a very successful company at the time, within a few years the man running the company and that insisted on firing Mark lost his health and then his life. The company totally went under. There is no longer a company existing.

Mark exhibited symptoms of MMD from a very early age. Throughout his life as health issues would arise, we, nor the doctors that treated him, ever suspected he had an underlying genetic disease. Mark would not and could not look at his condition as a terminal illness. I guess this was the only way he could deal with it without being depressed all the time.

As we dealt with Mike, it was a huge blessing that Mark seemed to be doing pretty well. About four years after Mike's death, Mark was visibly getting worse. He had a very quiet personality, and never complained, but I could tell things were beginning to change. His lungs were getting progressively worse. I dreaded the winter months, because I knew even a cold could very quickly turn into bronchitis and then pneumonia. Mark was very frail, weighing about 125 pounds. He only had one biological child, a son, Erik. Thank God, Erik was spared the disease, so it can go no further down through Mark's children.

On December 31, 2013 as my husband, Joel, and I were preparing to go to a New Year's Eve party at our church, the phone rang. I answered the phone and it was Erik, my grandson. "Maw-maw! I just got a call! My dad's not breathing!" were the words spoken.

"What happened?" I replied.

"I don't know, Maw-maw." Erik said.

"I am on my way. I will be right there!" I felt numb as I answered. I knew Mark had been sick for about a week with the flu that was hitting so many people in our area. He had been in bed for most of the week. He hated a lot of attention, so I tried to stay in the background and only be there when needed. After losing Mike, I found myself in panic mode each time Mark would get bronchitis.

About a month earlier, Mark's wife Carol called me one morning and said, "Mark really gave us a scare last night." I asked what happened and she related the story. She had gone to bed and was not yet asleep when she heard something at the door. She looked up and there was Mark, visibly in distress! He could not make a sound and she immediately knew he was choking. Just as she reached him, he was passing out.

147

She managed to put her arms around him from behind as he was falling. Carol did not know how to do the Heimlich maneuver, but she knew something needed to be done, and quickly. She did the best she could and managed to get the food dislodged. She was afraid she might have injured him internally from trying so hard to help him, so she put him in her van and took him to the emergency room. They checked him out and he seemed to be fine. When she finished telling me what happened, I said, "Carol, Mark's disease is beginning to progress. He really needs to have only soft foods. His throat muscles are getting weaker and there may come a time when he cannot swallow at all." This was something she did not want to hear. When I talked to Mark later, he told me he knew he was about to die, and he asked God not to take him then. God heard his prayer!

My husband entered the door and I said, "Something is wrong with Mark, he's not breathing!" We jumped in Joel's truck and all I could think was, "God, please let him be okay!" We live about fifteen miles from him and I was so scared. I knew he was frail and he had just had surgery on one of his eyes. He was scheduled for surgery on the other eye in a couple of weeks. I think Mark knew he was sicker than we realized, but he did not want to give up on life. He lived in the moment and that was a good thing for him. It must be horrible to know you will never grow old. After Larry passed and I sold our home, I bought Larry's parent's home and let Mark and Carol live there. He was very happy there since it is out in the country and is very quiet and peaceful.

As we neared the road that turns off the highway, I

148

could see the ambulance coming and I knew it was Mark. I told Joel to follow the ambulance. He was taken to the local hospital and we were right behind them. As we came through town, police cars were blocking traffic to let the ambulance through. One of Mark's good friends worked with the sheriff's department; somehow I think he learned something had happened to Mark.

As they opened the back of the ambulance, I saw my son lying on the stretcher. The first thing I noticed was his stomach moving and I thought, 'He's alive!' Erik and Carol were getting out of their car and without thinking, I blurted out: "He's breathing!" He was not breathing. The EMT crew was bagging him to pump air into him.

Carol wanted to collapse, but I would not let her. I told her she had to hold it together, Mark needed us right now. I really could not deal with her going to pieces on me at that point. I did not even know what happened! They rushed him into the ER and as Carol went in to give information, I turned to Erik and asked, "What happened?" Erik was in a state of panic, but mumbled, "He choked! He's been unconscious for an hour. It took the ambulance thirty minutes to get there!" He continued, "I was just there, and he was fine!"

The EMT's could not get a pulse or revive him. I knew he was probably already gone. We waited, and finally, we got word they had got a heartbeat. Even with a heartbeat, they said he was totally unresponsive. He probably had severe brain damage with his brain going for an hour without oxygen. I knew in my heart the prognosis was grim.

149

The doctor finally called us back into a conference room and told us Mark was alive and they were air-lifting him to Hattiesburg to Forrest General Hospital. The doctor knew how grim the situation was and asked if we would like to have a word of prayer together, so we did. Everyone, including the doctor, prayed for Mark.

We immediately left for Forrest General Hospital, in Hattiesburg, Mississippi. On the way there, I kept going over all of the what-if's. I was praying for God's will; not necessarily for Mark's life. I knew Mark could not deal with the long term situation with ventilation and constant care we had experienced with Mike.

Mark was in a room and when we went in to see him, I knew the chance of him coming out of this was very slim. He was still completely unresponsive. They had packed him with ice to try to conserve any remaining brain function. He was so cold and even though his heart was beating, I did not feel he was really there. I just felt a deep sense of loss and helplessness. There was absolutely nothing I could do. I prayed but it seemed futile. I knew Mark would not want to be here with severe brain damage, so I asked God to please not leave him here with that outcome.

We went to the waiting area and our pastor had arrived. Everything seemed surreal, like I was in some kind of dream I could not wake from. We sat there and talked, but it was mechanical for me. I really did not want to talk. I just wanted to go somewhere by myself and cry. How do you come to terms with something like this? How do you give up your loved one? I guess at this point, I felt no hope.

The time to visit came and as I entered the ICU cubicle, Mark was just there. I talked to him, but I knew he could not hear me. He was so cold. His body temperature had dropped too low and now they were trying to increase it to warm him up. After Carol walked out, I looked at the nurse and said, "There is not much hope, is there?" He looked back at me and I could tell that he knew there was not much that could be done, but he could not tell me that.

We decided since we did not know how long we would be at the hospital and we may have to take turns staying, everyone left except Carol and me. It was a very long, exhausting and mentally challenging night. After the 6:00 am visit, I told Carol to go to my car and get a little rest. I went in alone on the ten o'clock visit and a different nurse was on duty. Again, I talked to the nurse. I knew he could not tell me much, but I was groping for some kind so hope. From looking at the monitors and seeing how erratic and unstable his heart rate was, I knew it would take a miracle.

God had given Mark back to me when he was five years old and I had him for forty five years. In my mind, I totally gave it to God! I cherish every moment I was privileged to have with my son. I was glad Larry did not have to witness both of his boys leaving this world. He was very close to his children.

I had been back in the waiting area for about an hour when the nurse summoned me to go back to the ICU. I knew something was happening and I did not feel it was good news. As I entered the room, the doctor was there and asked who I was. I told him I was Mark's mom and he asked if I was the one making decisions

151

concerning Mark. I informed him his wife was resting and I could get her if needed. The doctor informed me Mark had suffered a major heart attack and he was expecting him to code any time. He told me to get Carol as soon as possible because they had to know her wishes about a ventilator. I went hurriedly to the car to get Carol. On the way to the ICU, I tried to prepare her for the worse.

As we were hurrying toward Mark's room, the doctor was in the hall. When he saw us, he came toward us and did not waste any time getting to the point. He immediately said to Carol, "Mrs. Smith, we need to know what you want us to do when your husband codes. Mrs. Smith, your husband is dying." He continued, "Your husband is severely brain damaged and we are expecting……" He did not get to finish his statement. We heard the alarms going off and I knew it was Mark! The nurses were running toward the room and the doctor turned again to Carol, "Mrs. Smith?" Carol looked at me and I just shook my head. She, too, shook her head no. The doctor rushed into the room and told the medical team to stop.

He was gone. We went into the room as the nurses were turning off the machines. The doctor gave his condolences and told the medical team to give us a few moments with him.

I went to one side of the bed and Carol went to the other. We held his lifeless hands and wept. Nothing was said for a few minutes and then Carol said, "Did you know Mark testified in church last Sunday?"

I looked at her in amazement and said, "No! Really?" Mark had never done that. He was so shy.

We had been having some conversations about God; I wanted him to be right with God. He told me he wanted to be baptized again when the weather warmed up. He was baptized when he was young and he had started going to a small church close to where they lived. I was elated to learn this new information. I needed a confirmation he was on good terms with God. I later learned from the pastor of that small church Mark had knelt between the benches and talked to God that day! How awesome! God knew He was going to call Mark home so He drew him close to Him to prepare him for his exit.

"I intreated thy favour with my whole heart: be merciful unto me according to thy word."

Psalms 119:58

Chapter 20

Rainbows

The rainbow is symbolic. It was designed by the Master to be a reassurance to the Earth that the world would never be destroyed by water again. You never see a rainbow on a clear, beautiful day. It only appears after a rain or storm. It never ceases to capture the attention of whomever gazes upon this beautiful array of colors! It always brings to mind the promise of God. It gives hope. Occasionally I have seen a double rainbow and I always stand in awe of the magnitude of God's love and mercy. I learned there are always two rainbows, but we seldom see more than one. I cannot help but think God has a rainbow in reserve even though we do not see it or know about it.

I have been through many storms, but I have been privileged to see a lot of rainbows. One of the most beautiful rainbows in life is the incredible love of someone who cherishes you. The real beauty of true love is that it is not fragile. It is strong, enduring, constant and selfless. It prefers to give rather than take.

Life goes on and you learn there is joy in the midst of sorrow. Another beautiful rainbow of life is beautiful friends who hurt as you are hurting. They help bear your pain and you feel the awesome love that wraps you like a cocoon. I have been blessed with some incredible people surrounding me through so many storms.

I have prayed for strength to help my grandkids who lost their Dad when they were so young and frightened about their future. Mike's oldest daughter, Whitney has always been exceptionally bright and Mike wanted her to have a good education. She graduated college in May, 2012, and is employed in a job that she loves. Her Dad would be very proud of the beautiful Christian that she has evolved into.

Whitney has always excelled scholastically and achieves the goals she sets. When she was a teen, she won a national contest and spent a week in Washington, D.C. with a trip to the congress and White House. Whitney graduated High School with Honors, then graduated Southwest Community College with a massage therapy degree. Whitney then decided she wanted to study Radiology. She applied to Jones Community College and was accepted on her first attempt. Two hundred students applied and only fourteen were accepted. She was in the top fourteen. From the top fourteen only two students were chosen to get hands on experience at some of the area hospitals. Whitney was one of the two chosen. After the first year of academics, she was able to work the second as well as continue her education. She graduated from Jones in May 2012. After spending some time in Florida, Whitney now resides in Louisiana. Whitney has the ability to do whatever she chooses. She is an avid photographer. We consider her a perfectionist. She is an awesome rainbow of achievement and determination.

Michael, Whitney's younger brother, is working and attending classes at the college that his dad and grandfather, Larry, attended. The former president of Southwest Mississippi Community College played college basketball with my husband, Larry. After completing two more years of college, Michael will have an opportunity to be employed with the college full time. My son would be so proud of his two wonderful children! The sun is peeking out and the rainbow is awesome!

When you have to live on disability, being frugal is a part of life. You get used to living a different lifestyle than the ordinary working class family. Mark had two step daughters, Ashley and Sarah in addition to his biological son, Erik. Erik has experienced many challenges in his life and has overcome much adversity.

He suffers from a bi-polar condition but he is also determined to be a winner. Erik is now married with a beautiful wife and daughter.

Mark was blessed with a granddaughter, Allysse, and three step-grandchildren who were his heart. These kids, Hallie, Callie and Gage loved him so much and they were traumatized when they were in the house while Mark was choking. I found out recently these kids had been saving their pennies and had been making plans for a while to go to Disney World in Orlando. Mark had insurance to meet his burial needs but due to limited funds he could not afford or get a large life insurance policy.

Some years earlier, though, he had taken out an accident policy. I remember him telling me about it and I told him he was pretty much wasting his money. Carol had lost the policy and could not remember the amount of the policy. She remembered the company and contacted them. They gave her the information she needed to file a claim.

She filed on this policy and she called me and said, "Mrs. Ann, that accident policy Mark had is going to pay."

I replied, "Really, how much was it?"

She told me the amount and I was very happy!"

What a beautiful rainbow! What Mark could not do in life, he accomplished in his death. He was unable to go to Disney World but he made it possible for those grandkids he wanted to take. Carol was able to purchase a home. A beautiful God Moment Miracle!

One of the most beautiful rainbows in my life is my amazing daughter Melissa. God insisted she come into our life. I look back over the last fifteen years and I do not know what I would have done without my Godly daughter and her kind and gentle husband, Baron. To say I love them would be an understatement. I remember when her dad died, how she took me, sheltered me and protected me with so much love and care. I remember the company Baron worked for wanted him to transfer to Florida. He was working in the New Orleans office at the time, and after Katrina, the company wanted to close the New Orleans office. Baron would make his offer to the company so high he knew they would not accept it. He did this for three years. When they felt it would be okay to leave me, they moved. What a rainbow!

I have watched my incredible daughter overcome so much in her life and in the lives of her children. She chose to homeschool her oldest son when the school system wanted to put him in special education after the second grade. So many learning disabilities can be overcome with specialized training. She chose to do this herself. She knew the statistics of special education. So many times the children are passed from one grade to the next without much help. Because of her determination for her son to have an education, she has been unrelenting.

This young man graduated high school and spent a year in California at Christian Life Bible College, in Stockton, California. He has become an awesome young man of God who is sensitive and compassionate. Melissa has taught him not to accept the status quo. Because of his amazing mom and dad, this young man has learned to reach beyond what he considers attainable

159

and reap results that most could not. Beautiful rainbows of achievement!

I remember getting a call from my daughter and the panic in her voice as she told me there was something wrong with Alissa, her second child. She said, "Mom, I really need you to pray for Alissa. I do not know what is happening. She crawled to my bed last night, and could not walk. I am taking her to Children's Hospital." As soon as I heard this, I went to my knees. I was devastated. I could not accept that something was wrong with my beautiful granddaughter.

Both her youngest children were put in casts when they were smaller, and she had been informed it was a possibility that Alissa would have to have surgery on her hip if it did not develop normally. I prayed as so many others did and when they checked her out, she was okay. We never knew what happened; we simply gave God the credit for touching her and the situation. She is fine and becoming an incredible young lady.

Another beautiful rainbow is Seth, Melissa's youngest child. He is exceptional in many ways. Again, Melissa was challenged with Seth as he had problems in speech early-on and they thought for a time he would not be able to speak at all. He has been in speech therapy most of his life and recently Melissa discovered, after very specialized testing, he has an auditory processing disability. When my daughter is faced with a challenge, she immediately starts figuring out a way to overcome the challenge.

She is determined her children will have normal, productive lives and she is teaching them that they can overcome and become productive. She refuses to let her children feel they are disabled. Seth has a brilliant mind, and I can see him becoming very successful in life. He can communicate, and has already overcome so much. Without the mom and dad that he has, he would not have been able to excel as he has.

My son, Matthew, is another inspiration of hope and has a very humble and loving spirit. He never fails to make the effort on Easter Sunday to be in church with me. He has to put forth more effort than most to do this. His mobility is very impaired and he is beginning to fall more frequently. When I see him limping down the aisle, I know it is not without considerable effort. His love for me is overwhelming and an incredible rainbow in my life!

I feel so blessed and I have had people say things to me like, "I don't see how you handle it," or "You are such a strong person," and I think to myself, and often say, "I have a big God and He knows all." He sees the big picture, and so often, I cannot. God is the giver and taker of life. Death is the storm and LIFE is the rainbow. Life on this earth is beautiful with its full array of colors but I imagine the eternal life is incredibly brilliant and breathtaking. The peace of knowing the Master is unexplainable. I feel I have a rainbow set before me each morning as I rise and take a breath of life.

I know there will be other storms I will face, and I will feel like the bird in the cleft of the rock as she hovers over her young to protect them. Just as the bird has complete faith the storm will pass and there is perfect peace in the midst of the howling wind and rain, I too, will put my complete trust in the Master. I know it takes the storms to see the rainbows.

161

One of the Godliest women I have ever known was Sister Nona Freeman, a missionary to Africa, who was affiliated with the United Pentecostal Church International. She gave her entire life to winning souls for God. The inserted email below appropriately describes life. The color black as we know, is not in a rainbow, but when most artists are asked their most important color, they will say, "black."

NOVEMBER 2013-From Kneemail/ Nona Freeman & Nona Freeman Book Sales: BLACK; THE MOST IMPORTANT COLOR TO AN ARTIST.

Kneemail feels to post this. Don't you marvel at the times you go through storms and how look back and see how God sustained you? We go through valleys not fully understanding why, or what the purpose is in the unforeseen future for our hurt and misery.

Since forming our Kneemail group in April 2000, we are privileged to know people from many walks of life by them contacting us for prayer. Some of these requests come from people who are very accomplished artists. Their works are so incredible until we are at a loss for words. Over the years we have had the privilege of watching a few of them as they prepare to use this marvelous talent entrusted to them. It would be easy to be envious of such a glorious talent.

Three in particular are very accomplished in their work. Several times we have watched them as they load their palette in preparation to transform a blank canvas into a work of beauty. It has never failed, each time on separate occasions, we noticed there is one particular color they each reach for first as they prepare to paint. One would think it is brilliant red, bright orange, heavenly blues, snow white or even beautiful pastels, but not so; it's always black. When asked, 'Why do you always select black first?" Each time we have been told by all three artists, 'Because it takes black to bring out depth to my paintings and to make them life. It they ever become what I need them to be, it has to be the black because without black my work will never be what it can be."

A supporter said, when this was shared with them, "Wow, that's so interesting, as a graphic designer I work most often in the digital medium of colors and I too can tell you the importance of having enough black in a picture. One of the very first things I do in working with a picture is usually balance the dark and light values, and almost without fail the dark is needed to increase and even if not, it requires proper anchoring of dark values for the light ones to look correct.

The same is true in our walk with Jesus. How great to know in the storms of blackness we have Jesus. Even though we don't understand now, we know this test will be a testimony in time to come. Right now it's all dark and bleak, but when the blackness clears away, we will understand it better by and by.

On behalf of Nona Freeman; BLESS YOU IN JESUS name!!

Just as in an artist's pallet, the color black is needed in our lives to shape and mold our character. The storms of life create in us more compassion for others who are suffering and teaches us to depend upon a higher power. In eternity we are promised no more tears and just as in the rainbow, the color black will no longer be needed.

It has often been said at the end of the rainbow there is a pot of gold. I have experienced my "pot of gold" not in the riches of this world or monetary blessings but in the blessings that were showered from above in the form of "God Moment Miracles." The pot of gold awaits those who choose to live the Christian life and make God the center of their existence.

> **"But the mercy of the Lord is from everlasting to everlasting upon them that fear Him, and His righteousness unto children's children."**
> *Psalm 103:17*

The Rainbow

I saw a rainbow, Oh what a sight,
The dark clouds parted, the sky was bright,
A promise was given a long time ago,
We would not suffer again with such woe.

A glimmer of hope I saw in each ray,
God is the Master, each and every day,
He watches our steps, keeps us from harm,
We have complete assurance without alarm.

As I looked toward Heaven, colors so bright,
I knew God was with me, in darkest night,
My heart could rejoice with amazing peace,
Storms would come, storms would cease.

As my head is lifted, my spirit is quiet,
I know in my heart that everything is right,
God takes all the hurt, sadness and grief,
He gives assurance, these things are brief.

Whatever comes, I can face with a smile,
I will join my loved ones in a little while,
They will be whole, not hurting or maimed,
Rays of the rainbow, they have now claimed.

By Ann Smith Hill

Contact Information
eMail: snannaann@yahoo.com
P.O. Box 257, Franklinton, LA 70438
Cell: 985-516-6521

Made in the USA
Middletown, DE
07 March 2022

62260210R00106